D0953102

Praise for *The Gig Economy*

"The way that work works has changed. Work is no longer where you go, it's what you do. Whether we're just entering the workforce or seasoned pros, this fundamental shift requires a change in how we think. *The Gig Economy* provides a blueprint for thinking, planning and succeeding as an independent in this new world of work. It contains valuable insight and exercises for those who want to better understand how the new ways of working impact them. Combining self-reflection, practical financial planning ideas, and immediate steps that can be taken today, Diane Mulcahy both inspires and guides readers who are navigating the new workforce realities. This book should be on every working-age person's shelf; well-worn, marked-up and referenced over and over throughout our new, independent careers."

—Billy Cripe, Chief Marketing Officer, Field Nation

Diane Mulcahy deftly covers the fundamental drivers of the Gig Economy, as well as the mindset and behaviors you'll need to succeed in this brave new world of DIY careers. Her research pierces our entrenched habits on what has kept us glued to the trappings of full-time jobs, and her wit liberates us with strategies for assembling a meaningful portfolio of gigs instead, along with a lifestyle that is unnerving as it is exciting. Read *The Gig Economy* to learn how to make work work for you."

—Danielle Duplin, Co-founder, TEDxBoston

How we work is changing, and that allows all kinds of people to really focus on making a life, and not just a living. *The Gig Economy* is a practical field guide for understanding these changes and navigating them with your greatest goals in mind.

—Dave McLaughlin, General Manager,
Eastern US & Canada, WeWork

THE Gig ECONOMY

DIANE MULCAHY

THE Gig ECONOMY

THE COMPLETE GUIDE TO
GETTING *Better Work,*
TAKING *More Time Off,*
AND FINANCING THE *Life You Want!*

AMACOM
AMERICAN MANAGEMENT ASSOCIATION
New York • Atlanta • Brussels • Chicago • Mexico City • San Francisco
Shanghai • Tokyo • Toronto • Washington, D.C.

This publication is designed to provide accurate and authoritative information in regard to the subject matter covered. It is sold with the understanding that the publisher is not engaged in rendering legal, accounting, or other professional service. If legal advice or other expert assistance is required, the services of a competent professional person should be sought.

Library of Congress Cataloging-in-Publication Data

Names: Mulcahy, Diane, author.
Title: The gig economy : the complete guide to getting better work, taking
    more time off, and financing the life you want / Diane Mulcahy.
Description: New York, NY : AMACOM, [2016] | Includes bibliographical
    references.
Identifiers: LCCN 2016023117 | ISBN 9780814437339 (hardcover) | ISBN
    9780814437346 (ebook)
Subjects: LCSH: Part-time employment. | Flexible work arrangements.
| Quality
    of work life. | Career development.
Classification: LCC HD5110 .M85 2016 | DDC 650.1--dc23 LC record available at
    https://lccn.loc.gov/2016023117

About AMA
American Management Association (www.amanet.org) is a world leader in talent development, advancing the skills of individuals to drive business success. Our mission is to support the goals of individuals and organizations through a complete range of products and services, including classroom and virtual seminars, webcasts, webinars, podcasts, conferences, corporate and government solutions, business books, and research. AMA's approach to improving performance combines experiential learning—learning through doing—with opportunities for ongoing professional growth at every step of one's career journey.

10 9 8 7 6 5 4 3 2 1

DISCLAIMERS

This publication does not provide financial, legal, or tax advice of any kind, and AMACOM, Diane Mulcahy, and any of their representatives cannot guarantee that the information is accurate, complete, or up-to-date. While we made every attempt to include information that is current, AMACOM, Diane Mulcahy, and any of their representatives make no claims, promises, or guarantees about the accuracy, completeness, or adequacy of the information contained herein. Nothing in this publication should be used as a substitute for the advice of a third party. AMACOM, Diane Mulcahy, and their representatives assume no responsibility to any person who relies on information contained herein and disclaim all liability in respect to such information. You should not act upon information in this publication without seeking professional advice.

The author has made every effort to ensure the accuracy of the information within this book was correct at time of publication. The author does not assume and hereby disclaims any liability to any party for any loss, damage, or disruption caused by errors or omissions, whether such errors or omissions result from accident, negligence, or any other cause.

Some names and identifying details have been changed to protect the privacy of individuals.

To Kevin
for traveling with me
on the road less traveled

CONTENTS

INTRODUCTION

Take this job and shove it.

—JOHNNY PAYCHECK

Five years ago, I created and started teaching an MBA course on the Gig Economy, which was still an emerging trend. The course gained immediate traction and was named by *Forbes* as one of the "Top Ten Most Innovative Business School Classes" in the country. Now the Gig Economy is a common topic in the media and has become part of the election cycle debates, but few people really understand how to navigate it to build a thriving, satisfying, and successful work life. This book, like my class, fills that information gap.

If we think of the current world of work as a spectrum, anchored by the traditional corporate job and career ladder on one end, and unemployment on the other end, then the broad range and variety of alternative work in between is the Gig Economy. The Gig Economy includes consulting and contractor arrangements, part-time jobs, temp assignments, freelancing, self-employment, side gigs, and on-demand work through platforms like Upwork and TaskRabbit.

Many of the topics in this book are based on what I teach, and many of the exercises are based on assignments that have helped my students succeed in the Gig Economy, and have led them to start new businesses, plan time off, restructure their finances, and begin to create lives that are more engaging, satisfying, and better aligned with their priorities.

The Gig Economy is still in the early stages of disrupting how we work. Only one generation ago, most workers could expect to be full-time employees in secure full-time jobs, working for just one or two companies over the course of their careers. The generation retiring now built a life anchored around the expectations of a stable and rising income, a steady package of corporate benefits, and a corporate-financed retirement at the end of work. That predefined climb up the corporate ladder is much less available to today's workers. That's how rapid the transformation has been. In just one generation, the corporate gravy train full of plentiful, progressive, benefit-rich, and secure full-time jobs has left the station.

The MBA students I teach today are facing a very different work world when they graduate. They don't expect security from one job. Instead, they plan to hold multiple jobs over the course of their careers, most likely for the median tenure of just three to five years each.[1] Their working lives will be made up of a variety of diverse work and work experiences.

They don't assume steady and increasing income. Wages are stagnating, and while working independently can generate higher earnings, it can also result in lower compensation.[2] Everyone wants to be paid well, but factors like flexibility, autonomy, and alignment with the mission and meaning of work are important to workers today, and many are willing to trade off some amount of economic compensation for jobs that offer those benefits.

They're also entering a world where workers are increasingly dissatisfied with the rigid structure of the traditional employee-in-a-job model. A 2014 Gallup poll found that less than one-third of employees are engaged and passionate about their jobs.[3] In fact, during the past decade, the majority of Americans haven't been satisfied with their jobs.[4] Surveys of independent workers, in contrast, indicate that they are more satisfied with their work, and more engaged.[5] They value the autonomy, flexibility, and greater control they have by *not* being a full-time employee, and in many cases they earn more.[6] The Gig Economy is a new way of work that seems to be working.

These changes have enormous implications about how we think about managing our careers and structuring our lives. The traditional arc of American life—graduate from college, get a job, get married, buy a house, have kids, send kids to college, retire—is still available, but it's more challenging to achieve without the solid foundation of a stable job and a steady and increasing income to support it. The Gig Economy offers more possibilities to arc our own journey and create our own path. As it continues to grow, we can expect the Gig Economy to change not only the way we work, but also the way we live.

How to Succeed in the Gig Economy

The intention of this book is not simply to educate you about the Gig Economy but to guide you through it and provide a toolkit for succeeding in it. All of the chapters have practical exercises to help you apply the concepts to your own life. The chapters are structured as independent modules, so you can read and focus on areas that interest you or matter to you most.

The question this book answers is: How do I *successfully* navigate the Gig Economy? The answers are broken out into 10 rules to succeed in the Gig Economy.

TEN RULES TO SUCCEED IN THE GIG ECONOMY

1. Define Your Success

Discover your personal vision of success, which might look very different from the traditional American Dream.

2. Diversify

Learn to identify and find gigs to increase your opportunities, improve your skills, and expand your network.

3. Create Your Own Security

There is no job security. Understand how to create income security, an exit strategy, and your own safety net.

4. Connect Without Networking

Decide if inbound or outbound connecting works better for you, and discover how to make great asks and offers.

5. Face Fear by Reducing Risk

Tackle the big fears that are holding you back, break them into manageable risks, and develop an action plan to overcome them.

6. Take Time Off between Gigs

We can expect to take a lot more time off in the Gig Economy. Here's how to plan for it, and make it meaningful.

7. Be Mindful About Time

Reboot your calendar to spend time on what matters. Consider whether a Maker or Manager schedule works best for you.

8. Be Financially Flexible

Forget the save-your-latte-money approach to money management. Restructure your financial life, and increase your financial flexibility and security.

9. Think Access, Not Ownership

Owning is so Baby Boomer. Access the things you want with less debt and more flexibility. Examine the myths of home ownership.

> **10. Save for a Traditional Retirement ... but Don't Plan on Having One**
>   Answer the question: When can I stop working?

Each chapter is dedicated to addressing one of the 10 rules—why it exists and how it's best applied. The book ends with a final chapter about The Future Gig Economy and how this new world of work might look for the next generation.

What's Driving the Growth of the Gig Economy?

There are two simultaneous and persistent trends driving the growth of the Gig Economy: full-time jobs are disappearing, and full-time employees have become the worker of last choice for many companies.

Full-Time Jobs Are Disappearing

The private sector used to create and add jobs to the economy at a rate of 2 to 3 percent per year. In 2000, during the dot-com crash, that rate fell below 2 percent. In 2008 the rate of job creation fell even further—below 1 percent—and has remained at that historically low level through 2015.[7]

One reason for this decline in job creation is that the engine of job growth has sputtered and stalled. It turns out that young businesses—not small businesses, as is widely believed—create most new jobs.[8] Age of the business is what matters, yet the growth of new young businesses has fallen by half, from 16 percent of all firms in the 1970s to just 8 percent in 2011.[9]

Even worse, the businesses that do start up are creating fewer jobs. Young firms used to create about 3 million jobs per year, but that number has fallen to barely over 2 million. The Ewing Marion Kauffman Foundation (where I am a senior fellow) refers to this phenomenon as the "long-term leak in job creation" in which "businesses have been starting in fewer numbers, with fewer employees, growing slower, and, therefore, generating increasingly fewer new jobs for the U.S. job market."[10]

In addition, companies are eliminating the full-time jobs they do have through layoffs, downsizings, and reorganizations. They are also taking previous full-time jobs and breaking them down into smaller projects or tasks to be automated, outsourced, or contracted out. It's cheaper, more flexible, and more efficient to do so. For example, newspapers have far fewer full-time staff jobs but much more freelance writing work available. In the Gig Economy, where there once were *jobs*, there is increasingly just *work*.

The Full-Time Employee Is the Worker of Last Resort

Full-time employees are the most expensive and least flexible source of labor for companies. The U.S. labor market is structured so that companies pay the highest taxes, and offer the most benefits and protections for full-time employees, which means that hiring an employee can cost 30-40 percent more than equivalent independent workers.[11] The Department of Labor has made no serious effort to alter this dynamic. Instead, it has chosen to preserve the status quo by increasing resources to identify companies that misclassify workers as contractors instead of employees, a Sisyphean task given the government's unclear, imprecise, and varying definitions of employee and contractor.

Not unexpectedly, the trend of hiring independent contractors instead of employees has become persistent and widespread, and it's growing. Companies incur lower labor costs, have more flexibility, and can realize greater efficiency when they purchase the labor they need by the project, by the task, and by the hour. For example, an employer can fill a former full-time marketing manager job with a part-time public relations person, a social media contractor, and an outsourced copywriter. They can precisely allocate and pay for work only when needed.

That said, the demand for full-time employees hasn't, and won't, disappear entirely. There will always be a core group of essential workers, in-demand talent, and senior management that companies will want to hire as full-time employees for various reasons—to secure specific talent and skills, fill high-touch, relationship-focused positions, or ensure quality or consistency in key areas of their business. Beyond that core, as long as our labor policies perpetuate meaningful economic differences between contractors and employees, demand for independent workers will continue to grow.

What Does the Gig Economy Mean for Employees?

The impact of the Gig Economy on workers depends on which type of worker you are. The Gig Economy is an economy of skills, and skilled workers are the winners who take all. Their talents are in demand, so they can command high wages and have the most opportunity to structure and design their own working lives and craft their own futures. They can take advantage of the chance to create a working life that incorporates flexibility, autonomy, and meaning. Skilled workers have the chance to move from good jobs to great work.

Middle managers and corporate wage slaves don't appear to be winning. Their skills are less in demand and more likely to be automated, contracted, or outsourced. Maybe they're hanging on to the final dangling remnants of the ladder they were climbing or clinging anxiously to the full-time corporate job they've managed to hold on to so far. Their income is stagnating, their benefits are shrinking, and they are too slowly coming to terms with the reality that they no longer have job security. These workers are surviving in their full-time jobs but struggling if they lose them.

The fate of retail and service workers and others in low-skill jobs changes marginally in the Gig Economy, but they continue to be the worst off. These workers are already in mostly poorly paid, insecure, part-time jobs with limited to no benefits, and no control over their schedule. Their wages are stagnating or declining, and their jobs are the most at risk of being automated. Zeynep Ton, an adjunct associate professor at MIT's Sloan School of Management, refers to these as "bad jobs."[13] These bad jobs won't go away in the Gig Economy; they are the persistent bane of our economy and our society.

The Gig Economy is not a silver bullet. It won't eliminate bad jobs and poorly paid workers, but what it can do is offer some positive change for these low-skill workers. In the Gig Economy, these workers have the chance to gain more control and have more flexibility and autonomy in their working lives. Uber drivers work under similar circumstances that most taxi drivers always have: they are contractors with no benefits, no overtime or minimum wage, and no access to unemployment insurance. But there are many more people willing to be Uber drivers than taxi drivers, in part because they can control when and how much they work. Similarly, the economic plight of an on-demand worker for a company like TaskRabbit or Postmates is not materially different from that of a low-wage hourly worker in a fast food restaurant or retail store. They both have low wages and no benefits, but workers who wouldn't dream of applying for a job in a fast food restaurant are willing to work on platforms like TaskRabbit or Postmates partly because they can do so when and how much they wish. The Gig Economy gives low-skill workers the chance to move from bad jobs to better work. It's not a big change, but it's a change in the right direction.

Is the Gig Economy Really New?

If we step back and consider the Gig Economy and its place in the history of work, we realize that it's not really new. There have always been contractor and consulting gigs, as well as part-time jobs. What *is* new is the spread of the Gig Economy into middle class and white-collar jobs, and into the business model of highly valued, highly visible technology startups.

THE MIDDLE CLASS: Contract and part-time work without benefits used to be largely limited to "bad jobs" in fast food, retail, and other service companies. Now that contractor work is infiltrating core middle-class industries, it's gaining more attention. An executive assistant used to be a good middle-class job. Now we can hire a virtual assistant, in the United States, India, or anywhere else, by the hour. If we want an accountant or bookkeeper, we can automate most of that function on QuickBooks or hire a contractor via Upwork, LinkedIn, or FlexJobs.

Universities already pay teachers by the course as adjunct professors, and those part-time, non-tenured faculty members (of which I am one) now make up a growing minority of teachers at many U.S. colleges and universities. How long will it be before this teaching model moves into our public school system? The more the Gig Economy demonstrates that white-collar and professional work can be restructured, contracted out, and purchased more cheaply, the more disruptive it feels.

TECHNOLOGY COMPANIES: Somehow, when we encounter part-time workers with no benefits at the local fast food drive-through or contract workers in our local taxi, it's less newsworthy than when we can beckon those same part-time workers and contractors on our phones and ask them to deliver stuff to us or drive us somewhere. Technology platforms like Uber and TaskRabbit that are built on contract labor models and achieve stratospheric valuations are much more compelling clickbait than a story about a regular taxi driver or someone's personal assistant. It seems like now that it's a tech story, labor is suddenly interesting.

The labor issues raised by the Gig Economy are not at all new. Back in 1995, the Department of Labor (DoL) deemed our labor market incentives perverse. They concluded that our current system encouraged employers to structure their workforce with contractors in order to realize the significant cost savings by avoiding the hiring of full-time employees:

> . . . current tax, labor and employment law gives employers and employees incentives to create contingent relationships, not for the sake of flexibility or efficiency but in order to evade their legal obligations. The employer will not have to make contributions to Social Security, unemployment insurance, workers' compensation, and health insurance, will save the administrative expense of withholding, and will be relieved of responsibility to the worker under labor and employment laws."[14]

It's been over two decades since that report, yet our labor policies have remained the same . . . even though they make less and less sense in a world where fewer and fewer workers have a full-time job with a single employer. The Gig Economy is an economy of work, but our labor policies only offer benefits and protections to employees who work in traditional jobs.

How Big Is the Gig Economy?

It's hard to know for sure how big the Gig Economy is or precisely how quickly it's growing. Normally, the responsibility for collecting data on employment and labor market trends falls to the Bureau of Labor Statistics (BLS). The BLS has so far done a poor job attempting to quantify the growth in the Gig Economy. Their last survey on contingent workers was conducted in 2005.[15]

Finally, though, a few recent studies provide early evidence that the Gig Economy is significant and growing rapidly. Economists Larry Katz from Harvard and Alan Krueger from Princeton conducted detailed analyses of tax data and found that:[16]

- ▸ The percentage of Americans engaged in alternative work increased by more than 50 percent over the past decade, from 10 percent in 2005 to 15.8 percent in 2015.
- ▸ The share of individuals filing Schedule C tax forms (the form used to report self-employment income and losses from operating a business or working as a sole proprietor) nearly doubled from about 8.5 percent in 1980 to just over 16 percent in 2014.
- ▸ Their most striking finding was that "all of the net employment growth in the U.S. economy from 2005 to 2015 appears to have occurred in alternative work arrangements," not from full-time jobs.

For now, an employee in a full-time job is still the dominant model of work but employers are moving away from that model and so are workers. There are fewer jobs being created, companies are hiring more contractors and part-time workers, employee benefits are declining, and many workers prefer to have greater autonomy, flexibility, and choice over their work. We still can't point to an exact figure that represents how many workers are currently working in the Gig Economy, but the evidence is clear that the number is steadily and rapidly growing.[17]

Stop Looking for a Job

The Gig Economy is disrupting how we work by transforming our labor market of jobs into a labor market of work. It offers both companies and workers an alternative to the one-size-fits-all model of a full-time employee in a full-time job.

For workers who are skilled, the Gig Economy provides opportunities to turn good jobs into great work. For less-skilled workers in traditionally "bad jobs," it offers the potential to turn those bad jobs into better work. By disaggregating work from a job, workers can realize levels of autonomy, flexibility, and control that have been traditionally unavailable to employees.

The Gig Economy is also disrupting how we live. Our traditional highly leveraged, high-fixed-cost lifestyle won't work as well in an economy of variable work and income. And structuring our lives to binge work for 40 years and then retire doesn't make as much sense when we can take more time off along the way and have a more balanced mix of work and leisure throughout our lives.

Succeeding in the Gig Economy requires a new mindset, specific skills, and an updated toolkit, all of which we'll cover in the next ten chapters. Succeeding, though, doesn't mean finding a job. It means creating a more aligned, better balanced life, and finding satisfying work that helps achieve your vision of professional and personal success.

So, stop looking for a job, and start creating your Gig Economy life.

Part One

GETTING
BETTER
Work

Chapter One

DEFINE YOUR SUCCESS

This is the beginning of anything you want . . .

—ANONYMOUS

Our earliest ideas of success come from others. It starts at home with what our parents and family think and then continues at school and work with what behaviors our teachers and bosses reward. We respond to these early influences by internalizing the versions of success we see around us. If we let them, these external versions of success can overwhelm our own visions, causing us to follow the well-worn path to a life that we might not want to live.

Brenna was leading a typical life of an MBA student. She was in her third year working at a Fortune 500 company in a job that made her feel trapped. She enrolled in the MBA program even though she preferred on-the-job learning to the classroom. And she was living at home with her parents in the suburbs, which she found dull, in order to pay down her student loans. She was pursuing a path based on external markers of success rather than her own vision and goals.

Brenna was my student, and after finishing my course (which was the first in her MBA program), she quit her job, dropped out of the MBA program, and moved into the city. When I caught up with her about a year later, she was working for a well-funded startup in a challenging role that aligned with her long-term interests, she was enjoying the convenience and ease of urban living, and she was engaged to be married. She still had not re-enrolled in the MBA program and wasn't sure if she ever would. Brenna had stopped living the life others expected her to and started following her own interests and desires. She created her own vision of her success.

If we don't take the time to reflect on what success means to us and what our version of it is, we can all too easily fall into living a life based on the priorities of others: how much time our boss thinks we should spend in the office, what our parents want us to study, and what career will impress our friends. If we haven't taken the time to reflect and be intentional about our priorities, we risk making decisions that deviate from what we truly want. We end up taking that lucrative job that requires a ton of travel when what we really want is time to connect and contribute to our family and friends at home. We work too much and too long, even though we say we want to prioritize raising our kids, training for the marathon, or hanging out with our aging parents.

To define success for ourselves, we must turn away from the external and cultural versions of success around us. Only when we quiet the peer, parental, academic, corporate, and social voices telling us what we "should" want and what we're "supposed" to do can we listen for our own internal desires and dreams. And only by listening carefully can we start to see what our version of success looks like.

Jessica Fox, a former storyteller at NASA and author of *Three Things You Need to Know About Rockets*, recommends a process that she uses to tap into her own thoughts and dreams called "playtime" (she reveals the interesting outcomes of this process in her book).[1] She describes playtime like this:

There should be a time of day, every day, when you're alone, when you put your phone down and, to quote my favorite author, Joseph Campbell, "simply experience and bring forth what you are and what you might be."[2] How you do that doesn't matter. You can just sit there and stare out a window, you can sketch, or you can see what images or words come up, and write them down. The point is simply to get in touch with your own thoughts. Something within that mire of ideas that comes out will be a seed or a germ that's incredibly important to you, that you wouldn't have had time to listen to unless you did this kind of exercise. Or something will come forth that's been in you but you're not listening to it. Sometimes you'll notice a pattern, something coming up over and over again. Pay attention to that. There's no need to create anything out of this, this is a time of creative incubation. You just see what happens.

Try taking some playtime, and then completing the exercise below.

EXERCISE

Define Your Vision of Success

To see that internal vision, start by asking yourself questions that will help you articulate your priorities:

- What does success look like to me?
- What are the values and priorities I want to live?
- What is my definition of a good job, a good career, and, even, a good life?

The answers to these questions will become your guide to the financial, professional, and personal decisions you make.

The New American Dream

Our American version of success has historically been tied to our vision of the American Dream: the house, the car, the 2.3 kids, and the leisurely retirement at the end. Yet there's some evidence that this image is changing. MetLife conducted 1,000 interviews for its *Study of the American Dream* and concluded, "Americans are less concerned with material issues, and that life's traditional markers of success—getting married, buying a house, having a family, building wealth—do not matter as much today. Rather, achieving a sense of personal fulfillment is more important toward realizing the American Dream than accumulating material wealth."[3]

The Center for a New American Dream survey of nearly 2,000 Americans reached a similar conclusion.[4] Their respondents named personal freedom, security, achieving personal potential, and having free time to enjoy life as their top answers to the question of what their particular version of the American Dream looked like. We're seeing a new version of success taking hold that is more focused on personal priorities. It's less about square feet in our home(s), the car(s) in the driveway, and dollar(s) in the bank and more about experiences, relationships, and personal fulfillment.

Research on what leads to a happy and meaningful life suggests that modifying the traditional American Dream to focus more internally and on personal fulfillment is a step in the right direction. Tim Kasser, a professor and the author of *The High Price of Materialism*, analyzed a decade of empirical data on materialism and its effect on our well-being. His research shows that focusing our lives on material pursuits breeds anxiety, isolation, and alienation. He found that placing a high value on material goods is associated with insecurity and lower levels of social and empathetic behavior. His research results suggest that organizing a life around our intrinsic values is the best way to increase our sense of well-being.[5]

The emergence of "digital nomads" is one example of this new, less-materialistic version of success. Digital nomads use technology to work, live, play, and travel when they want, from where they want. Freed from commuting, cubicles, the suburbs, and the status quo, they build geographically flexible lives around the places they want to be. It's the antithesis of the traditional life centered on an office building, a mortgage, and a commute between the two. Unconcerned with what "everyone" thinks they "should" do, digital nomads are creating lives defined by their own version of success and working according to their own rules.

Harness the Power of Hindsight

Hindsight is a useful tool for reflecting on our life choices and how we might make them differently going forward. The Harvard Study of Adult Development, started 75 years ago, has been following a group of 724 men throughout their lives. The study uses hindsight to help us understand what has mattered over the course of its subjects' lives. Its biggest finding was:

> . . . many of our men, when they were starting out as young adults really believed that fame and wealth and high achievement were what they needed to go after to have a good life. But over and over, over these 75 years, our study has shown that the people who fared the best were the people who leaned in to relationships, with family, with friends, with community.[6]

In the end, money and career success didn't correlate to greater happiness or meaning—only relationships mattered.

With similar results, hospice nurse Bronnie Ware summarized the regrets she heard most frequently from people at the ends of their lives. She found that people were most disappointed about their failure to prioritize internal priorities over external markers of success: "I wish I'd had the courage to live a life that was true to myself, not what others expected of me" was the most common regret.[7]

If only we had the foresight of our hindsight, we could make better decisions. In the absence of that, these three thought experiments attempt to harness the power of hindsight to home in on our internal vision of success.

EXERCISE

Refine Your Vision of Success

STEP 1: THE OBITUARY EXERCISE

The traditional obituary exercise asks you to write down the obituary you would like to see written about yourself when you die; it's meant to be an aspirational review of the life you would like to have lived.[8] The following obituary exercise is similar, but it asks you to write two obituaries: one that reflects the life you're leading and one that reflects the life you aspire to lead.

Roz Savage, author of the book *Rowing the Atlantic*, was a 33-year-old management consultant in London when she sat down and wrote the two versions of her obituary. She reflects on the impact it had on her life:

> The first was the life that I wanted to have. I thought of the obituaries that I enjoyed reading, the people that I

admired. . . the people [who] really knew how to live. The second version was the obituary that I was heading for—a conventional, ordinary life—pleasant and with its moments of excitement, but always within the safe confines of normality. The difference between the two was startling. Clearly something was going to have to change. . . . I needed a project. And so I decided to row the Atlantic.

Roz decided to go live the obituary she wanted to have. She sold her house, left her job, and started a new life. She is now an author, speaker, and environmental activist and has rowed solo across the Atlantic, Pacific, and Indian oceans.

STEP 2: THE DASH EXERCISE

This is a twist on the obituary exercise based on the poem "The Dash" by Linda Ellis.[9] The title refers to the dash between the date that you're born and the date that you die.

> "For it matters not, how much we own,
> the cars . . . the house . . . the cash.
> What matters is how we live and love
> and how we spend our dash."

Take the challenge of the poem to consider: How do I want to spend my dash?

STEP 3: THE VIRTUES EXERCISE

David Brooks, in his *New York Times* article "The Moral Bucket List," notes that American society spends more time teaching and rewarding us to develop our *resume virtues* than our *eulogy virtues*.[10] "The resume virtues are the skills you bring to the marketplace. The eulogy virtues are the ones that are talked about at your funeral—whether you were kind, brave, honest or faithful. Were you capable of deep love?" For this exercise, reflect on:

- What virtues do I spend most time developing in my life and why?
- What eulogy virtues would I like to cultivate?

Defining our vision of success is not a one-time exercise. It's one we should revisit routinely throughout our lives. We're usually in our teens and early 20s when our first vision of our adult life starts to form. It's then that we start building a life around what success looks like and map out a plan for our future: Law school! A 10-year slog to partner at the firm! A big house! A family and a dog! Then, 20 years later, we've made partner, hold the title and the degree, and live in a five-bedroom house with our family and the requisite dog but feel dissatisfied, unhappy, and unfulfilled. "Is this all there is?" we wonder. We're in our 40s and on the verge of a midlife crisis because we're living with decisions we made two decades ago, when we had different values and experiences to draw upon. We never stopped along the way to check in, reflect, reconsider our choices, and make changes to our vision.

How do we avoid this trap and, hopefully, the crisis? Richard Shell, a professor at the Wharton School of Business at the University of Pennsylvania, advocates that we take "pit stops" along the way to accomplishing our goals in order to evaluate our priorities and our varying definitions of success.[11] This means that we need to check in, reflect, and recalibrate regularly. We should—both on our own and then together with a partner or close friend—stop to reflect and update our definition and go back through this chapter to review and respond to the list of questions again. Our answers are likely to have changed, and, if so, we'll need to course correct.

These "pit stops" should be frequent because research shows that we are very poor predictors of what our future selves will enjoy, be happy about, and find meaningful. Daniel Gilbert, a professor of psychology at Harvard University, has found through his research that we are poor predictors of how our future selves will feel in any given situation.[12] When we imagine what might make us happy or fulfilled or how we might feel in different circumstances, we're mostly wrong. Gilbert found that one of the best ways to figure out what we like, what we enjoy, and what makes us happy is to observe and ask others who are already doing it.

This process of observing and asking people who are already in the situation we're contemplating is called *surrogation*. It sounds incredibly simple, but Gilbert's research shows that just asking other people about their experiences doing the thing we want to do improves our ability to predict our future experiences by 30 to 60 percent over our own reflection, research, and con-templation. The reason surrogation works is because we all share a common and broad base of likes, preferences, and reactions to events. As Gilbert notes, "Everybody prefers a weekend in Paris to being hit over the head with a two-by-four."

Surrogation can help us define and refine a vision of success that is most likely to be fulfilling. By identifying people who have achieved our version of success, we also give ourselves role models and a possible path we can follow to achieve our vision. We likely already know or are aware of people who we think are successful. Consider who they are and what they've done that makes them successful in your mind.

Surrogation and Success

STEP 1: IDENTIFY SUCCESS

Who do I know and consider successful?

- Identify and write about five people I consider successful.
- What specifically makes me think of them as successful?

STEP 2: PRACTICE SURROGATION

Can I meet with them to ask about their experiences achieving success?

Success Is Contagious

While we're looking in our networks for successful people, it's a good time to also take stock of the people closest to us and who we spend the most time with. Nicholas Christakis and James Fowler, professors at Harvard, spent significant time mapping the social connections of the 50-year-long Framingham Heart Study, which has followed more than 15,000 people over the course of their lives. The study offers evidence that behaviors and attitudes spread socially among groups of friends and even friends of friends. They called this phenomenon "social contagion" and found that smoking, drinking, obesity, happiness, and even loneliness appeared to spread socially. They also document how creativity, wealth, political views, violent tendencies, and happiness spread through social networks.[13] The authors concluded that we're influenced not just by the attitudes, feelings, and behaviors of our immediate circle of friends but also by people within three degrees of separation from us (i.e., our friends' friends' friends).

Jim Rohn, a personal development expert, famously noted that we become the average of the five people we spend the most time with.[14] Stop and consider for a moment who your five people are. Do they reflect your vision of who you want to become?

Rohn's theory also reflects the idea that we're heavily influenced, whether we realize it or not, by the behaviors, thinking, and attitudes of the people closest to us. The lesson is, if we want to achieve our vision of success, it helps to surround ourselves with people whose priorities and vision are aligned with ours (we'll talk more about how to intentionally connect with others in chapter 4). We might define our version of success, but the people closest to us play an important role in helping us achieve it.

The Timeline of Success

The time frame we set to realize our goals influences whether we achieve our vision of success. We might not be able to start our own small business and write our debut novel next year, but we can probably accomplish one, or even both, during the next five years. Nigel Marsh illustrated this concept best during his popular TED talk "How to Make Work-Life Balance Work."[15] He emphasized the importance of selecting the right *time horizon* for evaluating whether we achieve work/life balance. He noted that "a day is too short; 'after I retire' is too long. There's got to be a middle way."

Marsh's point is that the time frame we pick to accomplish our goals can impact whether we achieve them or not. In his example, we might not be able to achieve work/life balance on a particular day, but if we extend the time frame to a month or to a year, we're more likely to be successful. The same concept applies to achieving our version of success.

Time horizons can help us better allocate all of our resources—our time, energy, attention, and money—to achieve our goals. We have to beware of our natural tendency to over-allocate our resources to short-term activities that offer immediate rewards instead of to our long-term goals and priorities. Clayton Christensen offers the most compelling illustration of the consequences of overinvesting in the short term. In his *Harvard Business Review* article "How Will You Measure Your Life?" he describes how, more than 30 years after graduation, many of his classmates have ended up "unhappy, divorced, and alienated from their children" even though none of them set out to do so. Too many of them spent too much time on short-term wins in the workplace and not enough time investing in the longer-term, harder-to-measure rewards on the home front. Christensen asserts that our overinvestment and over-allocation of time and energy to short-term goals puts our longer-term goals at risk. To overcome this tendency, we need to keep our long-term goals "front and center" and consciously allocate our resources to them.[16]

Why Is It Either/Or?

Time horizons are also powerful because they can help us avoid false dichotomies—choices that look like *either/or* decisions in the short term but are really *and* decisions within a more generous time frame. For example, if I'm a self-employed consultant, I might find myself deciding whether I want to *either* spend the summer off with my kids *or* work during the summer to achieve my financial goals for the year. In the short term, the choice is *either/or.* But if I extend the time horizon and plan to spend *next* summer off at the beach, I can use the year in between to save money, take on additional clients to generate more revenue, and give advance notice to existing clients that I'll be taking off next summer. By allowing myself the additional time to plan and execute those three steps, I can do both—spend the summer on the beach *and* achieve my financial targets for the year. We can accomplish more of our biggest and most meaningful goals if we give ourselves the right amount of time.

This question of *either/or* versus *and* isn't a concept that applies only to time horizons. It's a framework that is useful to challenge our assumption anytime we're faced with any choice. It forces us to examine more closely if any given choice is real or false. Let's consider the most common dichotomy: Should I do what I'm passionate about *or* what makes me money? Rather than operate within this limited choice, why not consider doing what you're passionate about during the day, as your primary activity, *and* take on a side gig that makes you money? Or vice versa: Work during the day *and* find your passion during non-work hours. By questioning why it is an *either/or* decision, we can challenge our assumptions and, in many cases, find a better and more satisfying *and* option.

Adopt an Opportunity Mindset

Succeeding in the Gig Economy requires us to work in different ways—not always as full-time employees—and to think about work differently by shifting from an *Employee Mindset* to an *Opportunity Mindset.*

The worker with the *Employee Mindset* seeks to answer: What job can I get?

The worker with the *Opportunity Mindset* seeks to answer: What work can I do, and what value can I bring?

A worker with an Employee Mindset wants, or even expects, an employer to organize, structure, and present a preconstructed job with a ladder to climb, and a predefined version of success at the top: the corner office, the title, the big salary. Workers with Employee Mindsets largely delegate their sense of security, financial stability, and professional development to their employers. They rely on their employer to help them realize success and achieve financial security. The Employee Mindset is relatively passive in nature and counts on an employer to organize and provide a predefined job with prepackaged benefits.

This mindset has persisted in part because companies were once willing lifetime stewards of an employee's career trajectory and financial security. Companies used to offer long-term secure jobs, regular promotions, raises, and benefit increases tied to seniority. They also rewarded workers with guaranteed pensions and healthcare benefits during their retirement. It was reasonable to rely on employers because they were reliable. Now that companies make no promises or guarantees, offer no sense of security, and increasingly avoid hiring full-time employees, maintaining the Employee Mindset is unrealistic and highly risky.

A less-risky approach to succeeding in the Gig Economy is to transition to the more proactive Opportunity Mindset. Workers with Opportunity Mindsets see themselves as active creators, builders, and architects of their own career trajectories, not the recipients of them. They accept and expect to generate their own customized version of security, stability, and identity that is separate from any one company or organization. They create their own visions of success and work to achieve it.

An Opportunity-Minded worker actively connects with others, learns new skills, and seeks out new experiences. Even when working as full-time employees, those with Opportunity Mindsets think more strategically about what skills, experiences, networks, references, and knowledge their current job can offer to position them for a better future. They try to determine what they can achieve and learn in their current role that is transferable for their next one. The Opportunity Mindset requires more effort than the Employee Mindset but is a much less risky one to adopt.

YOUR DEFINITION OF SUCCESS IS
THE NEW AMERICAN DREAM

Greater flexibility in the way that people can work, as a contractor or freelancer or in traditional full-time jobs, is increasing our options and augmenting our choices about what success looks like and how to achieve it, allowing us to dream and creatively build our lives around our priorities and values. There are many versions of the new American Dream and what success looks like. In the Gig Economy, we are each more free to pursue our own.

As you think about defining your own version of success, consider:

- ► How can I better define and refine my own version of success?
- ► Do I surround myself with people whose vision of success is aligned with mine?
- ► Have I selected the right time horizon for achieving success?
- ► Have I adopted an Opportunity Mindset?

Chapter Two

DIVERSIFY

You can't model for the rest of your life, so it is important
to diversify your career.

—TYRA BANKS

Allison trained as a classical opera singer. She majored in voice
performance and Italian literature in college, but before she even
graduated, she knew she would not pursue a career in opera. Her
passion for it had dwindled over the past two years, and she
realized her passions and abilities were far broader than the
world of opera. She knew that she had to come up with another
plan. After graduation, she leveraged a college internship into an
entry-level job at the Israeli consulate, the first of several jobs she
would hold in international relations. Today, more than a decade
after graduating, Allison has combined the talents that led her
to opera, the performance, singing, and breathing skills she
learned during training, and her international work experience
into a portfolio of three gigs:

1. Allison is an entrepreneur. She founded and runs her own
   public speaking firm that helps clients around the globe find
   their voice and learn to be better and more confident public
   speakers. She incorporates breathing techniques and tips about
   being on stage and performing into her work with clients.

2. Allison teaches public speaking and communications as an adjunct lecturer at Georgetown's business school and at the Kennedy School of Government at Harvard University.

3. Allison taught herself to play guitar and is now a folk singer. She has recorded two CDs and performs live around the globe.

What Allison has done is what the Gig Economy requires of us to succeed—leverage our existing skills, experience, and interests into a diverse portfolio of multiple gigs. Diversification is the new normal of the Gig Economy. Diversifying our work reduces our risk, opens up new opportunities, expands our networks, and develops our skills. Diversifying our interests brings balance and variety to our lives and gives us a way to explore our passions, nurture new interests, and satisfy our curiosities. Like Allison, we can be the public speaking coach *and* the folk singer. We have the freedom to have multiple identities and the chance to focus on both personal and professional goals.

Management thinker Charles Handy described the idea of a diversified portfolio career as "a portfolio of activities—some we do for money, some for interest, some for pleasure, some for a cause."[1] Portfolio workers were individuals who purposefully chose to build a diversified life of multiple roles and projects, both paid and unpaid. They could accomplish personal and professional goals and achieve a balance between money and love, play and work, passion and pragmatism.

Diversifying creates security. *Top Chef* judge Gail Simmons realized the power of diversification when she left her full-time job as the director of events at *Food & Wine* magazine. She had started judging on Bravo TV's reality show *Top Chef,* and it was taking off. The success of the show and the time she spent on it led her to negotiate with the magazine to move into a consultant role. This shift allowed her to take on new projects that over time would include hosting *Top Chef: Just Desserts*, brand consulting (recipe development, brand ambassadorship, and media consulting) for a variety of companies, writing a book, teaching, and sitting on the Board of Directors for several nonprofit and for-profit organizations in the food space. Gail has also started her own production company and her first show, *Star Plates*, aired on the Cooking Channel. Gail believes that in the Gig Economy, "work is about the hustle. You have to create your own destiny." In Gail's view: "I actually have way more security than 95 percent of my friends because I'm so diversified. My income comes from ten to twenty places every year, so if one thing goes away, I don't have to worry."

Building a Portfolio of Gigs

Diversifying means building a portfolio of different gigs. The most common approach to building a portfolio is to start with the gig that pays. For many readers, a full-time job or a significant contract assignment is the anchor gig of the portfolio. Most jobs are short term (median tenure is less than five years for most age groups) and all jobs are insecure, so that gig will change over time. Adding other paying gigs can increase our sense of security and limit our financial downside by providing an income cushion.

But not every gig in the portfolio has to be, or even should be, one that pays. Gigs don't have to generate income to deliver value. They can be projects or volunteer positions that allow us to explore an interest, learn a skill, rekindle a passion, cross something off the bucket list, or simply participate in an activity that gives us joy. The reasons for pursuing any given opportunity vary as much as the opportunities do. Almost every gig will help us develop and hone our skills, expand our networks, and position us for a future opportunity. Gail Simmons majored in anthropology and Spanish in college because those were the subjects she enjoyed and was interested in, but, as she says, "I've come to realize, 20 years later, that food is anthropology. What I'm really most interested in is how food is a window into culture. . . . And how we eat is so indicative of who we are." Anthropology turned out to provide a strong foundation for her interest in food. Of her major in Spanish, she points out that she works in the food industry in New York City. "What's the language of the kitchen?" she asks. That's right: Spanish.

We can't always tell what gigs, what skills, or what experience will matter most to us later or will prepare us for the perfect opportunity. The best we can do is follow our interests and curiosities and do our best to satisfy both. As you consider how to build your own diverse portfolio of gigs, think about including ones that help you do the following:

Gigs to Get Your Foot in the Door

Many of us dream of doing something with our lives that looks completely different from what we're doing right now, but we're not quite sure how to make the transition to break into a new field. If that's the case, find a gig that offers the opportunity to begin the process of meeting, interacting, and forming connections with people in a new industry or sector.

For example, Katherine was working full time at an advertising agency, but she constantly found herself sketching the perfect living space in her head. Her true passion was interior design, not advertising. Katherine had no contacts, network, or experience in the design industry, but she had plenty of determination, so she went out and got a part-time job working weekends at a high-end furniture store. This gig gave her a way to begin establishing connections in the local interior design industry. She got to know her colleagues, many of whom were well-connected designers, and she met designers who came into the store to shop for clients. Just by being around other interior designers, Katherine was able to ask questions and start learning the basics of the business: how to pitch clients, how much to charge, how to scope and manage projects, and what the common mistakes were. After working at the store for a while, Katherine was hired by her first client. Less than a year later, she left her full-time job and started her own interior design firm, which is still going strong. Her part-time job in retail was her foot in the door to learning a whole new industry and launching her own business.

Gigs to Experiment

Having a portfolio of gigs allows us to create low-risk opportunities to experiment with new ideas and new opportunities. An experimental gig lets us test an opportunity and if we find we don't like it, we can drop it and try something else. By using gigs to create small pilot tests of opportunities, we create the option to either continue and invest more if it's successful or stop and move onto something else if it's not. We limit our investments of time, money, and resources yet still obtain valuable information and learn about what worked and didn't, what we liked and disliked.

Jill is a good example of someone who experimented through a side gig. Jill was in a fast-paced corporate legal position in New York City. After a decade at the same firm, she felt it was time to move on and was considering moving from the corporate world to working with startups. To explore the entrepreneurial ecosystem, she started by attending a Startup Weekend and working alongside a group of entrepreneurs to develop and pitch a business idea. She rented a short-term desk in a coworking space as a way to meet entrepreneurs. She began acting as a pro-bono legal adviser to several startups, which helped her become familiar with the legal problems they faced and develop experience solving them.

Jill ultimately decided to return to working for a large company, but her experimental work with startups broadened her business and legal skills, expanded her network, and gave her more professional career options. Jill's example illustrates that side gigs don't have to develop into full-time positions to be considered successful. Instead, they can give us valuable information to make better decisions about our next steps.

Gigs to Learn by Doing

We can build a portfolio of gigs that gives us opportunities to learn on the job, at our own pace, in lower-risk situations. For instance, when I first became a part-time adjunct lecturer, I was a nervous and novice public speaker. The idea of getting up at a professional conference and speaking to a large audience of colleagues was very stressful to me. Yet I felt relatively less stressed and safer in front of a group of students, teaching a course I created, and talking about a subject I knew well. Through my side gig as a lecturer, I practiced speaking every week that I taught class, and I was able to experiment with a variety of speaking techniques, find my own voice, and request feedback from colleagues and students. By the time my day job required me to take on more public speaking responsibilities, I was practiced and comfortable enough to smoothly transition to that role. My gig as a lecturer gave me the chance to learn public speaking by doing it.

Gigs to Do What You Really Want to Do

We can build a portfolio of gigs to make sure we do the things we've always wanted to do and help us avoid the deferred life plan. *The deferred life plan* refers to our tendency to focus first on things we "should" do or are expected to do, while deferring the things we really want to do until. . . someday (which may or may not arrive).[2] Living the deferred life plan is risky. There's a significant chance that we'll get so caught up in the identity and trappings of the life we're leading (the title, the compensation, the position) that we'll later find it difficult to separate ourselves and step away to do the things we want to do.

We also expose ourselves to the possibility of goal creep. For instance, we assure ourselves that we'll work as a corporate lawyer or investment banker until we hit our number (the amount of money we want to have), but half a decade later we're completely caught up in the lifestyle and the number we think we need to achieve starts getting higher. The constantly moving goalpost of the ever-increasing number means we'll never feel satisfied enough to stop what we're doing and shift to what we want to do. A portfolio of gigs can help us avoid deferring our lives by giving us a way to pursue the things we really want to do starting today.

Finding Gigs

Everyone's portfolio of gigs is different, based on their interests, their goals, and what they enjoy. As you think about building your own portfolio, try to consider a wide range of potential opportunities that accomplish both professional and personal goals:

- ▶ Part-time jobs, either in your current industry or, like Katherine, in a new field

▸ Advisory or board positions you take to apply your skills differently or to expose yourself to new industries/sectors

▸ Nonprofit or volunteer work you do out of interest or a sense of purpose

▸ Teaching a class at a university, through an adult education organization or online, or teaching a skill like skiing, pottery, knitting, or a language

▸ Starting a small business on the side consulting in your area of expertise or selling products (your homemade jewelry, your delicious candy bars) or services (your editing help, your college coaching assistance) unrelated to your primary work

Shari has implemented a deliberate approach and strategy to building a diverse portfolio of gigs. She likes to think of her portfolio as made up of several buckets. She described four specific buckets that she tries to fill outside of her day job:

1. **BUCKET #1 holds volunteer board work.** Shari chooses companies she wants to work with, lending her business-consulting skills free of charge, and becomes a part of their decision-making committees. She looks for mission-driven organizations that align with issues that are important to her. Interestingly, the experience and exposure she gained from volunteering as a member of one nonprofit board led to a paid position as a board member for a company she wanted to work with.

2. **BUCKET #2 is for consulting clients.** Shari does short-term projects for a few clients. There is a known fee and time commitment involved.

3. **BUCKET #3 is the "sweat equity" bucket.** Here, Shari parcels out who on her list of contacts she has time to advise on their early-stage companies. This work is generally unpaid, but Shari enjoys working with entrepreneurs and startups and being part of that ecosystem.

4. **BUCKET #4 is reserved for Shari's personal attempts at starting companies.** So far she has given one solid effort at her own startup and it failed, but that hasn't kept her from returning to the drawing board.

When she looks back over her career, Shari maintains, her buckets of gigs "have been more valuable than anything I have done full-time and gotten paid a lot of money to do." She finds that her personal value is greatly augmented through the "skills, network, and exposure" her portfolio of gigs gives her. Diversification has helped her create opportunities, build skills, expand her networks, and spend time doing things she cares about and enjoys.

EXERCISE

Finding Gigs

Thinking about your own interests and goals, create ideas about what a diverse portfolio of gigs looks like for you.

STEP 1: IDENTIFY YOUR BEST GIG

Reflect and recall:

♦ What was my best gig? What about it did I love?

The best gig could be as far back and as simple as a great summer job you had during college, and it doesn't have to be for money.

STEP 2: IDENTIFY YOUR IDEAL GIG

Imagine the answer to:

- ◆ What would be my ideal gig?
- ◆ Why?
- ◆ What are the specific elements that make this my ideal gig? For example, is it the opportunity to be creative? To be in charge? To work from the beach? To immerse myself in an activity I enjoy?

STEP 3: DISCOVER POTENTIAL GIGS

Think about and answer:

- ◆ Write out 10 potential gigs that you could do and would want to do. Make sure to include some ideas that aren't money making.

The reason to write down at least 10 is that most of us can quite easily come up with 3 or 5 ideas. Real creativity comes after that, when we stretch beyond our immediate networks and comfort zone to find ideas outside our box.

This exercise is best performed by yourself and then with someone else—your significant other, a colleague or mentor, or a like-minded friend. Other people see us differently than we see ourselves and see possibilities for us that we might miss. It's also powerful to share our ideas. We can't anticipate the ways that others can contribute to moving our ideas forward.

The Risk of Over-Diversification

One question to consider when building your portfolio of gigs is, how much is too much? How many gigs should you have? You want to be careful to realize the benefits of diversification but not over-diversify. The easiest way to think about diversification concretely is to use a simple financial example. If you had a total of $25,000 in savings, you wouldn't invest it all in one company. There are too many reasons, none of which you can control or accurately predict, why the company could perform poorly, leaving you worse off. Lack of diversification is risky.

But what happens if you over-diversify the portfolio and invest ten dollars each in 2,500 stocks? It turns out that over-diversifying can be just as bad; it may constrain your losses, but it also limits your gains. Excess diversification eliminates the risk that any one company's poor performance will tank the portfolio but also limits the gain you'll realize from any outperformance. Over-diversified portfolios generate average returns that mirror, rather than outperform, the general market because the performance of any single stock doesn't meaningfully impact the performance of the whole portfolio.

We risk over-diversification if we spread ourselves too thin and do too much. If we over-diversify, we risk achieving less than we hoped and expected. We put ourselves in a low-risk, low-reward situation. We underinvest in every activity, which increases our risk of mediocre outcomes.

It's only worth making the investment in an activity if we can invest the right amount of time, energy, and attention to realize a meaningful reward. The challenge for each of us is to find the right level of diversification for ourselves.

Can We Diversify and Build Expertise?

Diversification has connotations of breadth, but it can also be deployed for depth. Malcolm Gladwell asserts in his book *Outliers* that it takes at least 10,000 hours of deliberate practice to obtain mastery in a cognitively demanding field.[3] But we can stretch out our 10,000 hours over the course of our lives, achieving mastery later in life. Or we can devote any single decade (i.e., our 20s, our 30s) to practice and mastery, which leaves many other decades left to dabble, explore, experiment, and pursue other interests. If we consider a long enough time horizon, we can achieve both mastery and variety.

Diversification can also provide us with information to help us decide where to specialize. This concept is baked into doctor training programs. During their internship, physicians rotate through multiple specialties, working for a few months at a time on each service, such as internal medicine, neurology, and cardiology, before selecting a specialty and becoming an expert in one practice area. They diversify in order to decide where to specialize.

We can also become more expert by diversifying how we apply our skills and knowledge. For example, I'm a part-time writer. This is my third book, and I've also written articles, book chapters, and op-ed pieces. If I wanted to expand my skills further, I could try my hand at an essay or take up blogging. I could work on a short story or perhaps experiment with another genre like fiction or mystery. I can deepen my expertise as a writer by diversifying the type of writing I do. By expanding into different styles and genres of writing, I become more expert in the craft.

DIVERSIFICATION IS
THE NEW CLIMB UP THE CORPORATE LADDER

Businesses reduce their risks and maximize their returns by diversifying their lines of business and revenues. Investors do the same by diversifying their portfolios. Yet when it comes to individuals, we're advised to concentrate: to work for one employer and generate one stream of income. This concentration is risky. Diversifying reduces that risk, and gives us the chance to develop new skills, expand our networks, and increase our future opportunities.

As you think about diversifying, consider:

- ► What are the ways I can build a diverse portfolio of gigs?
- ► What kind of gigs would I like to include in my portfolio?
- ► What existing skills, networks, and knowledge can I leverage to create new gigs?

Chapter Three

CREATE YOUR OWN SECURITY

Security is mostly a superstition. It does not exist in nature, nor do the children of men as a whole experience it. Avoiding danger is no safer in the long run than outright exposure.

Life is either a daring adventure, or nothing.

—HELEN KELLER

Michael worked for 30 years at the same company before retiring at 55. Over the decades, he worked his way up from his entry-level job to management and never considered looking for another job or moving to a different company. He never really needed to; over time, there were enough opportunities where he was to move up, increase his salary, and build a nice nest egg with his company-funded pension. Why go elsewhere?

Kieran is in his 40s. He's a partner in a small consulting firm and an adjunct lecturer at a local university, and does executive coaching on the side. Kieran's career path has been anything but linear. He's moved from consulting, to a Fortune 500 company, to being an entrepreneur running his own company, and back to consulting. He never considered staying, or planning to stay, at one firm for his career. He's been able to do more, and make more, by changing jobs and moving companies. His nest egg, in the form of a 401(k) and IRAs that he funds himself, follow him wherever he goes.

Planning a career like Michael's is now both risky and unrealistic. Jobs aren't secure, getting ahead is based more on skills and knowledge than seniority, and putting every financial egg in one company's basket seems downright reckless. Having a portfolio of work and multiple sources of income, like Kieran, provides income security, work security, and some measure of financial stability.

There Is No Job Security

A job is no longer a viable foundation on which we build our professional, personal, or financial lives because jobs are no longer stable or secure. Companies are going out of business more frequently than ever. The average life of an S&P 500 company was 67 years in the 1920s, but it is just 15 years today.[1] That's not even long enough to have a career. A recent analysis by the Santa Fe Institute of 25,000 public companies found that the typical half-life of a public company is about a decade.[2]

The largest blue chip corporations that were once bastions of stability are now frequent instigators of layoffs, downsizings, and restructuring of their workforces. Firms are bought, are sold, and merge in transactions that routinely cull employees to realize cost savings and "synergies." In 2015, the rate of corporate layoffs continued to increase and included companies such as Microsoft (7,800 workers),[3] Proctor & Gamble (6,000 workers),[4] JP Morgan Chase (5,000 workers),[5] American Express (4,000 workers),[6] and Target (2,250 workers).[7] Walmart and McDonald's, the largest employers in America, both laid off hundreds of corporate jobs.[8] Even high-growth technology companies aren't immune. Twitter, Snapchat, and Groupon all conducted layoffs in 2015.[9] These cuts may generate returns for shareholders, but they eliminate any sense of job security for workers.

Traditional bastions of stability, like government work, teaching, and academia, still exist and offer relatively higher levels of security, but even those industries are under pressure. In 2011, one third of all layoffs were government positions.[10] Contract teachers, adjunct faculty, charter schools, and online education are disrupting the formerly steady jobs in academia. And the pensions that offered long-term financial security are in serious trouble. City and state pension plans that provide retirement funding for government workers and teachers are underfunded by more than $3 trillion.[11] There are increasingly fewer places to get a job if your goal is to find an employer that will provide you with any kind of job security.

Many people have trouble accepting the fact that there is no job security. Glassdoor, an online employer review site, conducts an Employee Confidence Survey every quarter in which it asks employees how concerned they are about being laid off in the next six months.[12] It also asks how concerned the employees are about their *coworkers* being laid off. Every quarter, many more employees—between 10 to 20 percent more—report being concerned about their *coworkers* getting laid off rather than themselves. This result could mean that the coworkers are incompetent slackers and are indeed more likely to be laid off, but it more likely suggests that the employees are in denial about their own likelihood of being shown the door. The Society for Human Resources Management similarly found that the majority (58 percent) of employees were not at all concerned about their job security, even though one-third (33 percent) of them reported that their company had layoffs within the past 12 months.[13]

Denial is not an uncommon strategy for dealing with job insecurity. We convince ourselves that it can't happen to us, that we won't be let go, and then fail to prepare for the possibility that our job status could change in an instant. A better approach, one that would help us feel more secure and less worried, is to assume that it *will* happen to us and take steps to prepare.

Create Income Security

Since jobs no longer offer security, we have to create it ourselves. The strongest security we can create for ourselves isn't job security, it's income security. If we feel confident that we can generate the income we need to support the lifestyle we want, we'll feel more secure, regardless of our current employment status. Security needs to come from our own skills and our own ability to obtain work and deliver value. There are a number of ways we can begin to create our own sense of security.

Create Income Security by Building Skills

The Gig Economy is a skills-based economy. More than degrees, titles, and other traditional markers of success, the new labor market is a market for the specific, demonstrable skills and abilities we can bring to potential employers and clients. We're also seeing a transition from a tenure-based system of employment to a skill-based one. Companies that used to reward seniority through promotions, better benefit packages, and pensions are now awarding compensation and titles based on an employee's ability to deliver outcomes and impact, not years at their desk.

Although each work experience gives us the chance to improve our abilities, knowledge, and expertise, we still have to proactively build our skill set independently of our day jobs.

Fortunately, it's never been easier (or cheaper!) to acquire and build a set of skills on our own. Our many options include:

- Taking individual courses through platforms like Coursera, EdCast, edX, NovoEd, and Udemy.[14]

- Building work experience and a reputation by using platforms like 99designs, Hourly Nerd, Topcoder, and Upwork.

- Improving social media and content creation skills by starting our own blog or Twitter account to share our views, knowledge, and expertise.

- Developing writing skills by self-publishing articles, an ebook or print book.

- Practicing speaking skills by taking a Toastmasters class, starting a podcast, or making a video on any topic we're interested in or knowledgeable about.

- Obtaining our own skills-based certifications: coding certificates, chartered financial analyst (CFA), certified financial planner (CFP), or actuary, insurance, or real estate licenses. These are just a few examples of credentials that can be obtained by passing a test and/or taking a course (often online).

- Fundraising through sites like Kickstarter, making it easier to pursue our creative, startup, or nonprofit ventures (Raise enough money and you, too, can record your own CD, manufacture that fun new widget, or launch a nonprofit to save the world).

The list goes on, but we can see that with so many low-cost and highly convenient options to learn at our keyboards, there's no longer any reason to rely on a company or a job to provide us the opportunity to build skills.

Create Income Security by Building a Pipeline of Opportunities

Even when we're fully employed, we still need to be alert for potential future opportunities by meeting new people, following work leads we're interested in, looking for interesting projects, and cultivating new gigs. Building a pipeline means that we're always looking and, more importantly, marketing ourselves for new jobs, projects, gigs, and assignments. Dorie Clark, the author of *Reinventing You* and an expert on personal branding, asserts that it's no longer just a job search, it's a permanent campaign:

> Many people don't want to deal with the hassle of a "permanent career campaign." They think it's too much work to contemplate their personal brand, maintain their social media footprint, or cultivate relationships when they're not on the make for a new job. Those are the people who will lose. Whether or not you want to play the game, it's happening around you.[15]

We are now part of the "hustling class," always looking for work, evaluating and updating our skills and value, and staying aware of potential future opportunities. We have to regularly scan the market to evaluate what changes are taking place, what skills are needed, and what value we can deliver. That way, when it's time to move on to our next job, consulting project, or assignment, we have up-to-date ideas about what we want to do next.

Create Income Security by Creating Multiple Sources of Income

We've seen how Kieran both is a partner in a consulting firm and does executive coaching. And how Allison runs her own company and is an adjunct lecturer. Having multiple sources of income, whether they come from working a side gig or leveraging an asset, like renting a spare bedroom on Airbnb, gives us a way to lower our financial risk, increase our sense of financial security and stability, and insulates us against the negative shock of a single event, such as getting laid off.

It can also be a low-risk way to launch and test a business idea. Instead of quitting our job to hang out a shingle, we can start slowly by testing the market, iterating what services we offer and what prices we charge, and then building revenues and customers on the side. Sharon started her own business as a side gig. She was working a day job in public relations, but her real love was writing. An author herself, Sharon was passionate about helping other writers succeed. She leveraged her writing and PR skills and started to run self-publishing workshops and discussions on how writers can pitch the media and create the awareness they need to sell their books. Attendees at her workshops saw the value of investing in someone with Sharon's expertise and started approaching her about running full PR campaigns to publicize their books. About two years later, Sharon has left her day job and launched her own firm focused entirely on public relations for authors. She sticks to the friendly, community approach: offering affordable rates and personal coaching for her clients. Her firm is thriving.

Create Income Security by Keeping Fixed Costs Low

The variable, changeable nature of work in the Gig Economy doesn't easily support a highly leveraged, high-fixed-cost lifestyle. It's difficult, risky, and stressful to commit to high monthly debt payments or fixed overhead costs if you don't know and can't rely on the amount of income you'll generate every month or every year. We discuss these topics in detail in chapter 8,

but—sneak preview!—creating a sense of income security requires us to rethink how we think about money.

Income security comes from keeping our fixed costs low and
manageable so the income needed to cover them is reasonably
easy for us to earn. When I interviewed independent workers in
the Gig Economy—from authors and speakers with lucrative
consulting gigs to freelancing recent graduates with lower levels
of income—they all emphasized the importance of maintaining
a lean financial life that their lumpy and variable income could
easily cover. Since all jobs are insecure, we can never fully rely
on maintaining a steady, level flow of income throughout our
working lives. We have plan for variable income, and keep our
fixed costs low to weather our changes in earnings.

Enter with an Exit Strategy

Creating an exit strategy forces us to consider and plan for what's
next. It ensures that we won't be blindsided and caught unprepared by a sudden layoff, downsizing, merger, or reorganization.
Knowing that we have an exit plan in place increases our sense
of security and control.

The crux of the exit strategy concept is to enter any commitment with the exit in mind. When we enter any commitment
with an exit in mind, it lends clarity to our decision-making:
We're less likely to feel trapped, and we're less likely to put ourselves in situations that limit, rather than expand, our options.
It might seem counterintuitive for those deeply embedded in the
Employee Mindset, but a good practice is to develop an exit
strategy to leave your job the minute you're hired.

In the investment world, an exit strategy is a common concept
to consider at the time you're making an investment. When you
buy a stock at ten dollars a share, you do so with a plan to sell it,

or consider selling it, when it reaches a price that gives you the return you're seeking. You buy the investment with the sale price in mind.

Having an exit strategy is also the norm in the startup world. When entrepreneurs are raising money from investors to grow their companies, they are asked about their exit strategies: Do they plan to sell the company? Take it public? When? Having an exit strategy doesn't mean that the entrepreneur isn't fully committed to his company, and the exit plan can change based on new information, but naming an explicit exit strategy at the outset ensures that everyone is working toward a common and defined goal and that milestones en route are clearly identified and measured.

Exit strategies can be created for just about everything in our lives. If you don't like your spouse, you can divorce (or consciously uncouple). Hate your soul-sucking commute to your toxic job? Sell your house or your car. Quit your job. Or do all three. Better yet, put a plan in place to do all three a year from now. Exit strategies are best executed with planning in advance.

We have the power at any time to wipe the slate clean and start over. Having that option does not minimize or diminish the effort, energy, loss, and high costs (emotional and financial) that can come with endings, closing of chapters, and transitions to a new phase of life. Exits can be painful, hurtful, difficult, and expensive. They can also be liberating, freeing, and full of possibilities. Whatever your situation, though, it's important to explicitly acknowledge that exits are possible (and inevitable) and to plan for them from the beginning.

Create an Exit Strategy to Leave Your Job

The fact that our jobs lack security creates insecurity. We worry and stress that we might lose our job and end up unemployed.

Instead of worrying, it's more productive to channel that energy into accepting that jobs are insecure and preparing to change work regularly.

Gig Economy workers need to know how to leave jobs well. We are not so much married to one company as we are serial monogamists (who date on the side!). We can expect to be in sequential short- to medium-term relationships with several firms over the course of our careers, in addition to our portfolio of gigs. We know to expect change. We might as well prepare for it.

The more practice we have building the skill of leaving jobs and moving on, the better at it we are, the more comfortable we are, and the less stressful it is. Leaving jobs is similar to moving homes. If we move infrequently, it can feel overwhelming and stressful. We feel entrenched in our current situation and may not even know where to start. We can't decide if we should keep all of our pairs of shoes or just 20 of them. We pack 50 books into a cardboard box and realize we can't lift it. When we move frequently, we learn what to do to make it easier, simpler, and less stressful. We learn to travel light and not accumulate too much stuff. We understand how to pack, and we learn what steps to take to make sure the process goes smoothly. The more we move, the better we are at moving, and the less stressful it is. Preparing to change jobs helps us whether we leave voluntarily by quitting or involuntarily because we're laid off.

Almost everyone dreams of quitting their job at some point. There are good reasons to quit: because there are no opportunities to advance, the learning curve has flattened, compensation or responsibilities have stagnated, or we've gained enough skills and experience to get a better role or better pay by leaving. We might be in the wrong job, at a toxic company, or work with a bad boss. There are also bad reasons to quit. Quitting impulsively or out of frustration can be harmful—it can burn bridges, damage relationships, and leave us worse off than if we had stayed.

The key in any scenario is to learn how to be a good quitter, and the way to be a good quitter is to plan ahead. Save as much as you can, be on a 'permanent campaign' for your next opportunity, and have a good exit strategy in place. Treat your employer well by giving ample notice and striving to leave on good terms. There's truth to the saying that you're only as good as your last gig, so positive relationships and strong references are worth preserving. We can expect to quit several times over the course of our careers. Learn to do it well.

Layoffs are a much more attractive exit than quitting because getting laid off is the only time we get paid to leave a job. Getting laid off from a professional job will generally include receiving a package of financial benefits to cushion the blow of job loss. Many firms will offer severance payments, payouts of unused vacation time, and any prorated bonus, as well as the chance to maintain health insurance through COBRA. Laid-off employees are also generally eligible to collect unemployment insurance for several months (the exact amount of time varies by state). These payouts may not equal our prior level of earnings, but they can provide a financial cushion while we find a new opportunity or accomplish other goals. If we find other work or another job right away, the cumulative payouts from a layoff can be an unexpected financial windfall. If we are unprepared or living above our means, any layoff or interruption in work can be devastating. But if we're prepared for change and if we have an exit strategy, getting laid off can be a positive experience and a window of opportunity.

To prepare to leave your own job, either by quitting or getting laid off, complete the following exercise.

EXERCISE

Create an Exit Strategy to Leave Your Job

STEP 1

Imagine that you are going to leave your job in six months. Create a list of tasks you would need to do to prepare. Make sure to address each of the following categories:

◆ **Professional:** What would I like to do next? What can I do now to start creating my next opportunity? What side gigs help position me for my next opportunity? What networking/connecting efforts should I start? Who should I contact?

◆ **Financial:** How much do I have to save? What opportunities can I pursue now to increase my income? What financial changes can I make to reduce my expenses, and how soon can I make them? What healthcare and other job benefits can I use before leaving?

◆ **Personal:** What changes in lifestyle, accommodation, or location would I have to make?

STEP 2

Review the lists of tasks from Step 1. Start doing them.

If you know people who have left their jobs and seemed to do it well, buy them a coffee and go over this exercise with them. What did they do to prepare professionally, financially, and personally for leaving? How would they prepare differently the next time? What are their recommendations, suggestions, and best practices?

Changing jobs every few years keeps us competitive. It forces us to consistently build new skills, expand our networks, and stay abreast of current market demands. Changing jobs can help us make more money. Particularly among younger workers in the first decade or so of their careers, changing jobs generates high levels of wage growth.[16] The reason is that once you're in a company, salary increases are generally limited to company norms, even if you're a high performer, so the best way to get the biggest increases in compensation is to change jobs.

Create an Exit Strategy to Reduce Uncertainty

When our future seems uncertain, instead of seeing opportunity for change, we can fall prey to certain cognitive biases that limit our ability to make the most of our situation. Paul Schoemaker, the author of *Profiting from Uncertainty*, identifies two cognitive biases around uncertainty that limit us. He refers to them as our "myopic eyes and timid souls."[17]

He asserts that we aren't clearly able to imagine, picture, and dream of the potential opportunities that arise from uncertain situations because we anchor on current information and over-weight information that is readily available. We have trouble seeing beyond right now, and what is right in front of us. These are our myopic eyes. Spending time creating exit strategies helps us overcome this myopia by encouraging us to imagine potential future opportunities as part of a deliberate and ongoing practice.

Our souls are timid because we are more sensitive to loss than gain and we have a very strong dislike of ambiguity. We prefer the steady job over the variable one, even when the rewards are greater in the variable one. In more concrete terms, that means that many people would choose a lower-paying steady job over more lucrative, but variable, freelance or consulting work. A good exit strategy is a defined, concrete plan that can lessen our ambiguity and embolden our timid souls.

Create Your Own Safety Net

Our labor market is structured so that employers are given tax incentives to provide their employees with benefits like health, disability, and life insurance and retirement plans. Workers who don't have a traditional full-time job and access to employer-provided benefits have to create their own customized and portable benefits package. Health insurance and retirement savings accounts are easy to access as an independent worker, and it's possible, but much more expensive, to purchase other common benefits in the private market. Many of these benefits vary by state, so you should assess your options by researching your own state's policies and offerings and working with a financial professional or attorney.

Healthcare: Accessing health insurance is one of the most important benefits to workers. The Affordable Care Act allows individuals to buy health and dental insurance through state health exchanges. The plans available and the premium prices vary by state. Subsidies to purchase health insurance coverage or the option to enroll in Medicaid are available if you qualify based on your income.

Retirement saving plans: This is covered in greater detail in chapter 10, but individuals can save for retirement by setting up and making contributions to retirement savings accounts. In additional to your contributions as an individual, you may be able to make an employer's matching contribution if you have set up a separate business entity.

Unemployment protection: Self-employed people and independent contractors aren't required to pay the federal and state unemployment taxes, so they aren't eligible for the unemployment benefits those taxes cover. Independent workers "self-insure" for unemployment, which just means they pay for it themselves by saving and setting aside a financial cushion for slow times.

It's worth noting that many independent workers aren't at risk of unemployment in the traditional sense. Prior to the emergence of the Gig Economy, losing your job meant going from 100 percent of your regular income to 0 percent. If your single employer laid you off, you had no job and no income. Now many workers have multiple streams of income—a short-term job, a side gig, Airbnb-ing their apartment—so if they lose their job, their income might fall to 50 percent of what it was, or 30 percent, but it would be rare that it falls to zero. The Gig Economy doesn't end unemployment, but it can mitigate it.

Paid leave (sick, personal, vacation): Independent workers decide when and how much leave to take, depending on their income goals and how well their business is going. Time off is not something they are *given* as a benefit, it's something they plan for and *take*. For example, when I lived in the Midwest, our local ice cream store was owned and run by a couple who worked like crazy during the busy warm-weather and summer months and then closed up shop every year from December through March—four months of annual time off. They were able to sustain that work schedule by creating a life that they could support on the income they earned only during the eight months they were open.

Similarly, Lauren is an independent consultant. It took her a while to figure out exactly the right setup, but after some tweaking she's settled on creating a yearly income goal that covers her expenses. She has chosen to set up a life that she can pay for with 10 months of income, which gives her a cushion to cover her expenses even when business isn't booming. In general, she sets an income goal that she thinks she can meet by October and sets her budget to stay within those limits. She usually knows by halfway through the year, in June, if she's on track to meet her income goal. That midyear check-in helps her figure out how much time she can take off during the summer and over the holidays. If she's running behind her income projections, she limits her time off and scales up her business development to try and close the gap during the second half of the year. If she's ahead of her income projections, good luck finding her in July and August!

Disability insurance: Like any insurance, you can purchase disability coverage in the private market, although individual policies are expensive. It can also be harder to get good coverage if your income varies significantly, and policies can vary based on what they cover (e.g., whether it considers you disabled when you can't do any work or when you just can't do your work), so it's best to talk with an insurance or financial professional to make sure you understand the details of the policy you buy. The silver lining is that if you purchase individual disability insurance and pay premiums with after-tax dollars, the benefits you receive are usually tax free.

Life insurance: Again, as with most insurance, you can purchase life insurance on the private market or possibly at a lower price through affiliation organizations (alumni organizations, professional associations). For readers early in their careers or just out of school, life insurance might be a less-important protection. Readers with dependents, whether they are aging parents, children, or a disabled family member, may want to prioritize continuous coverage.

Workers' compensation: Workers' compensation insurance is available if you work for an employer; otherwise, if you're harmed on the job, your only real option is to bring a lawsuit. You can't buy workers' comp on the private market. If you structure yourself as a business and hire any employees, you may (depending on your state and business) be required to purchase worker compensation insurance.

In addition to the traditional corporate benefits package, full- and part-time employees receive numerous protections that contractors and independent workers don't. Employees are covered by minimum wage and overtime rules, have protections against workplace discrimination, harassment, and injury, and are often covered under the Family Medical Leave Act. These protections are unavailable to independent workers.

If we engaged in a thought experiment and designed a benefits and protections system for workers today from scratch, we would never require workers to have a single employer and traditional job to access them. When reviewed in the light of day, our approach to providing benefits to workers is hopelessly outdated, inefficient, and collapsing. This inflexible system can keep workers locked into jobs they don't like just to access key benefits, and it forces employers to structure their workforce around obligations to provide and pay for benefits. The effort required to restructure this system for the demands of today's workforce is monumental but necessary.

In the meantime, we're already seeing some innovation and new options from the private sector to help independent workers create customized benefits packages. Peers.org is a startup that helps workers organize à la carte benefits packages, including health, vision, and dental insurance and retirement benefits. It also promises to help workers consolidate benefit contributions from disparate income streams. The Freelancers Union, Stride

Health, and Honest Dollar are other organizations and startups that are creating online platforms and solutions to help independent workers access benefits. As the Gig Economy continues to disaggregate workers from jobs, we can expect to see more demand and more options emerge for purchasing customized and portable benefits.

INCOME SECURITY IS THE NEW JOB SECURITY

To access the complete package of benefits, rights, and protections, workers must have a traditional full-time job. Yet jobs are insecure and unstable. That means workers must create their own sense of security through their ability to generate income and their own safety net of benefits from what's available in the private market.

As you think about creating your own security, consider:

► Have I accepted the reality that there is no job security?
► How can I create income security?
► Do I have an exit strategy for my current job or work?
► How strong is my safety net, and how can I make it stronger?

· Chapter Four ·

CONNECT WITHOUT NETWORKING

The most exhausting thing in life, I have discovered, is being insincere.

—ANNE MORROW LINDBERGH, *Gift from the Sea*

Friendly introductions and warm leads are the currency of the Gig Economy. We rely on other people to think of us, refer us to potential work and projects, mentor us, and connect us to institutions, colleagues, and companies that offer us new opportunities. If we want to create any movement or change in our lives—such as finding a new job, relocating to a new city or neighborhood, or entering a new industry—it's easiest with the help of other people.

We know to expect constant change in the Gig Economy. Jobs are insecure, and variable work is increasingly common. We're always on the lookout for new opportunities, side gigs, and possibilities for work, so our networks and connections are essential to our success. It's difficult to rely solely on a compelling résumé or being heard above the persistent noise of social media. We're better off cultivating our connections and networks of people who know us, like us, and can help point us toward good opportunities.

A good network is both deep and broad. Mark Granovetter, a sociologist at Stanford, best described the benefits of both in his seminal paper "The Strength of Weak Ties."[1] Our deep connections come from what he calls *strong ties*. They are limited in number and are the people we know best and interact with most frequently, like spouses, close friends, and current colleagues. Strong ties are important emotionally and are essential as the backbone of any fulfilling life. But, according to Granovetter, they aren't a good source of new ideas, perspectives, and opportunities because they are composed of people who are too similar to us. Our strong ties exist in the same orbit and world as we do, they know the same people, and they share too many of our perspectives.

Having a broad network is important because it introduces the benefits of *weak ties* into our lives. Weak ties are acquaintances, not friends. They are the colleague you met a few times working on a project together or the neighbor you run into occasionally on the street. You know them and have something in common, but you don't interact frequently and aren't emotionally close. It turns out that weak ties are the key to new opportunities. In his research, Granovetter looked at how people found new jobs. Less than 20 percent of those new opportunities came from strong ties; the remaining 80 percent originated from weak ties. For most of us, deep connections to friends and family will come naturally. Our weaker ties must be cultivated and maintained.

Inbound Connecting

When most of us think about networking, we imagine ourselves in large conference rooms with a glass of bad wine and a bunch of strangers trying to figure out who we should talk to. A better way to approach connecting is to skip those events and apply the digital marketing framework of inbound and outbound marketing to connecting.[2] Traditional inbound marketing relies on potential customers being "pulled" to the company by interesting and relevant content the company creates. Once potential customers arrive, the company attempts to convert them to customers.

Inbound connecting similarly relies on "pulling" people toward us through the content we create. There are multiple ways to inbound connect: writing articles, blogging, being active on social media, speaking at conferences, or hosting events. Through these platforms, other people can seek us out, connect with us, and begin a relationship. Inbound connecting favors introverts who may prefer fewer in-person interactions and appreciate time to think about their positions and views before sharing them.

Inbound Connect Through Writing

Stop for a moment and reflect on the newsletters, articles, and publications you read in your industry. You can probably identify some well-known experts simply because you read their articles, newsletter or monthly column. In my industry of venture capital (VC), writing has become such a popular way to build the brand and reach of individual VCs and their firms that there are now hundreds of VC blogs. Data company CB Insights has even culled and categorized 89 of the most active ones into The Periodic Table of Venture Capital Blogs, as a resource to the industry.[3] Writing is a powerful way to engage with others, start and join conversations, and connect, yet it's often underrated as a networking tool.

Writing doesn't need to be daunting. You don't need to start with a book or even an article. It can be as brief and limited as becoming active on Twitter, crafting 140-character tweets that engage you in conversations, publicize and support the work of others, or present your point of view. You can work your way up to more substantive pieces like writing articles, starting a news-letter, or blogging.

The easiest way to begin writing is to follow the three Cs, in order:

STEP ONE: Curate. The goal of this step is simply to iden-tify and start following the people and conversations that you enjoy and think are interesting. Look around on social media and in industry publications to find the people whose views you think are thought provoking and the conversa-tions that you enjoy tracking. Curating is an ongoing activ-ity, not a one-time event.

STEP TWO: Comment. Once you've curated interesting people and conversations, listen for a while. Observe the topics, how often people interact, the tone of the conversa-tions, and who the leaders are. When you feel like you understand the topics and tone and have something to con-tribute, join the conversation by commenting. Engage with bloggers and journalists by writing thoughtful comments on websites, respond to their tweets, and offer interesting links to articles. The goal of this step is to enter the ecosys-tem and begin to interact and engage in a thoughtful and substantive way. Most writers welcome intelligent remarks, questions, and observations about their work and are open to engaging with readers who provide them.

STEP THREE: Create. The final step is to create your own original content around the topics and conversations that interest you. What perspectives, points of view, or analysis can you contribute to the conversations you've been fol-lowing? You can share your content through a blog post or Twitter discussions. Social media is the easiest place to start, since we can push our own publish button and start a digital conversation on any topic with just about anyone.

Articles can take more work to publish, but their broader reach can be worth the additional effort. If you're a more natural speaker than a writer, record every talk you give and then get it transcribed. Almost any talk can serve as the rough draft for an article. If you're a natural talker, speaking is an easy way to segue into writing. Once you have an article, decide if it makes sense to publish your work on a general news site or if you should target industry-specific publications. Either way, seek to publish on the best-quality platform you can. Reach out to editors of your top-choice sites first and submit your piece. If your preferred publications aren't interested in publishing your article, work your way down your list until you get an acceptance.

Writing can be an effective way to increase your exposure, raise your profile, and generate other opportunities like speaking gigs. By establishing yourself as someone with a point of view, a perspective to share, and something to say, you become a person that others want to connect with. You shift from being the person writing the comments to the person receiving them.

Inbound Connect Through Speaking

Susan Cain is an introvert. She is the author of *Quiet: The Power of Introverts in a World that Can't Stop Talking*, and her "bliss" is writing, researching, and reading. Yet she is the speaker of one of the most popular TED talks, with over 13 million views. How did she do it? As she describes it, she overcame her lifelong fear of public speaking (which many of us share) by spending a year training and practicing.[4] She calls it her "year of speaking dangerously," and it involved Toastmasters, coaching, and practicing every chance she could. It worked. Susan's story illustrates key steps when starting to speak: Start small and practice.

Let's hop off the TED stage, though, and return to that earlier image of the endless evening of networking in a big conference room. Now imagine that you were a speaker at the event, not merely an attendee. All of a sudden, the image changes. There you are, holding your glass of cheap wine, and other attendees are approaching you and seeking you out. No more trolling around trying to decide who to talk to or how to break into an existing conversation. The connections come to you. It's a powerful shift.

Being a speaker at an event also automatically connects you as a peer to all the other speakers. Many events even host separate speaker dinners or speaker receptions to facilitate those connections. Being a speaker is the easiest and most effective way to meet, engage with, and connect with all the other speakers at your event.

The three Cs of writing also apply to speaking:

> **STEP ONE: Curate.** Like the curation step in writing, the goal is to familiarize yourself with your industry speaking events, the regular speakers, and popular topics. To do so, attend conferences and networking events and get a sense of what the topics are, who is speaking, and who is in the audience. Evaluate the skill level of the speakers and the range of speaking formats (individual talks, with or without PowerPoint, panels, roundtables, interviews, etc.). Get a feel for which events would be comfortable speaking venues for you. Sometimes it's easier to envision starting to speak at smaller, niche events than at large, industry-wide conferences.

STEP TWO: Comment. Commenting is a mostly underused approach to connecting with speakers. If you enjoyed someone's speech or found what the person said interesting or thought provoking, follow up with post-event comments to the speaker in an email or on Twitter. Usually after a speaking event there is a crowd of people around the speakers, asking questions and exchanging business cards. That's not the time to engage in a substantive conversation or expect to make a memorable introduction. Instead, use that time to get contact information for the speakers if it's not available in their bios or easily found online.

Save your substantive follow-up for after the event, when you have the speaker's full attention and you're not one of the crowd. Send a thoughtful email noting the most interesting points you took away from the speaker's comments. It's been a surprise to me as a speaker that surprisingly few audience attendees take the time to follow up after an event with substantive comments and a well-formulated ask. Be one of those few people. It will get the speaker's attention and most likely get you a response.

STEP THREE: Create. There are two ways to approach speaking gigs. The first is to focus on preparing to be a panelist, which requires you to have a clear area of expertise or a well-defined position in the industry and a few interesting perspectives or talking points that you can share on your subject. The second is to prepare to give a complete talk or an individual speech, which means building a PowerPoint deck or writing out the story you want to tell. If you're naturally a writer and you've already been publishing articles and perspectives, it might be easiest to turn an article into a talk. The flow and arc of writing and speaking can be similar.

There are still a few more steps to get your speaking gig. Once you have a topic or talking points in mind, assess your speaking skills. Some people are natural public speakers and enjoy being on stage. The rest of us are like Susan and deal with nerves, stage fright, and a general fear of speaking in public. This fear can be conquered with practice. Seek out relatively safe opportunities to start speaking. Look for the chance to talk in front of small groups you know well or give a short talk at a nonprofit you care about. Offer to guest lecture in a local university class, or give a small talk about your industry at career services. Start wherever feels most comfortable and build your speaking skills from there.

Once you feel confident that your speaking skills are up to snuff, start by reaching out to friends and colleagues who speak to let them know you're interested if they hear of any opportunities. Most regular speakers are asked to speak at more events than they can possibly attend, and it's helpful to refer the organizer to another speaker. You can also reach out directly to the conference or event organizers to express interest in being a speaker or panelist. In both cases, identify the topics you'd be qualified to discuss and disclose your level of speaking experience so you can be referred to the right types of opportunities.

Inbound Connect Through Hosting

Similar to speaking, taking on the role of the host or organizer gives you more visibility than being an attendee, which makes it easy to connect during the event and helps people remember you afterward. It also allows you to curate. If you're organizing and deciding the guest list and inviting any speakers, you can identify and connect with people you want to meet or get to know better.

Jayson Gaignard, author of *Mastermind Dinners*, has laid out a plan for how to maximize the potential of organizing your own events.[5] Jayson started hosting dinners of four to six curated guests. The dinners were purposeful and carefully constructed around people he wanted to meet and get to know and people who those initial guests referred him to. His goal was to build his own network and help connect people. Since starting to host the dinners, Jayson has become an evangelist for the power of connecting and purposefully networking. He credits the dinners and the people he met at them for his professional success.

Events you host can be large gatherings, small dinners, or even one-on-one meetings. Dorie Clark, the author of *Stand Out*, suggests hosting your own small networking event by inviting one or more people to join you in a specific activity, such as attending a professional event together or taking a lunchtime walk. The key is that the event is on your terms and involves an activity that you enjoy and are comfortable with. Rather than just meeting for coffee, events like these are more attractive to the people you've invited because you've offered to create and organize an experience for them.[6]

We might never completely eliminate the big rooms and the bad wine, but by inbound connecting through writing, speaking, and hosting, we can try to minimize them.

Outbound Connecting

Outbound marketing is when a company "pushes" its message to the market using all the channels we normally associate with marketing: online and traditional advertising, conference sponsorship, sales calls, and email blasts. Potential customers are generally involuntary recipients of outbound messages, so this method relies on reaching large numbers of people and generating a very small hit rate, or response rate. We can think about connecting the same way.

Outbound connecting is traditional networking. It's when we go to conferences and networking events hoping to meet people and "push" our message to them. Outbound connecting favors the extrovert who enjoys attending these events, meeting new people, and marketing themselves to others. If you enjoy outbound connecting, here are some more targeted and effective ways to approach it than just attending large events.

Outbound Connect by Joining Curated Groups

If you want to outbound connect in a more targeted way, start or join a curated group. Curated groups are smaller, selective events organized around a mutual interest (e.g., a running group or a book club), a shared affiliation (e.g., as alumni groups or neighborhood associations), or a common network (e.g., invitation-only events where you must be nominated by an existing attendee, such as TEDx). Curated groups make connecting easier because you start the interaction with a common bond or interest, making it more likely that you'll find an authentic way to connect to people who are a good fit with your personal or professional lives.

Outbound Connect by Leveraging Technology

Outbound connecting used to be a numbers game, kind of like dating. You put yourself out there, go to networking events and conferences, and hope you meet interesting, likable people. It can be a hard slog because the "hit rate" of meeting someone relevant at any given event can be low.

Technology is now transforming these events and providing attendees with the tools to make quality connections even at large events. Huge conferences like South by Southwest (SXSW) are now using apps like SXSocial that give attendees the ability to create their own profile, pick the best sessions to attend based on their interests, and integrate with sites like Facebook to help identify potential connections who are also at the event. Large industry conferences are using apps that give participants the ability to access the list of attendees and speakers and private message attendees in advance to schedule meetings. By the time they arrive at the event, attendees can already have a customized schedule, a list of meetings, and online introductions to other attendees. This technology is helping turn big conferences into targeted, efficient, and curated opportunities to connect.

Outbound Connect by Creating Your Gig Economy Pitch

Job titles used to be an easy, shorthand way to convey where we were in our careers and what our skills and competencies were. Everyone understood what a partner at a law firm did or what being VP at a local corporation meant. In the Gig Economy, our stories can be more complicated, but the goal remains the same: to tell people about ourselves in a way that is memorable and likable and helps people connect with us. We want to pitch ourselves in a way that is compelling and authentic.

When entrepreneurs are raising money or acquiring customers for their startup, they are advised to craft a verbal elevator pitch that summarizes their business and value proposition. The name comes from the imagined scenario of meeting someone important to your business in an elevator. The challenge is to have at the ready a compelling pitch for yourself or your business or ideas that can be delivered in its entirety during the elevator ride. Like elevator pitches, a personal pitch is a compelling statement that conveys your value proposition and skills.

- ▶ **Traditional pitch**: I'm a VP at an investment bank.
- ▶ **Gig Economy pitch**: I help companies raise the money they need to finance their growth.

The difference is that the traditional pitch relies on a static title while the Gig Economy pitch emphasizes what value you deliver, and to whom. The challenge of the Gig Economy pitch is to consolidate and summarize your varied work experiences into a single compelling pitch:

- ▶ **Bad Gig Economy pitch**: Listing all your marketing gigs and projects over the past several years.
- ▶ **Better Gig Economy pitch**: "I help technology companies explain what their product is and the problem it solves so they can recruit the right customers, investors, and employees."

Designed to be brief, personal pitches give us the chance to connect the dots and communicate the common themes in our narrative.

The Offer and the Ask

Whether we realize it or not, the basic way we connect with others is through offering and asking. We offer our help to someone, and they reciprocate by offering theirs when we need it or ask for it. We offer support and cheers for their accomplishments, and they offer the same for ours. It sounds mechanistic on paper, but it's not in real life. After all, this is how communities have always been built. I offer you a cup of sugar when you run out, you give me an egg when I'm short. Eventually, over time and transactions, we become good neighbors and then good friends.

Our offers and asks, just like our neighbor example above, can also lead to deeper relationships over time. For instance, when I met Jessica, her first question when we sat down for coffee was, "What are you working on that you're excited about?" That might not strike you immediately as an offer, but it was. She was offering me the chance to bypass the usual introductory small talk—what do you do, how long have you been there, blah, blah, blah—and move right into an authentic, substantive, and more personal conversation. I eagerly accepted and we had the first of many fun, interesting, and engaged conversations that led to us becoming friends.

Similarly, when I recently ran into an acquaintance, she asked me if I knew anyone on the nominating committee for a local award. When I asked why, she said that she knew of a local company that was doing great work and she wanted them to get recognized for it. She was hoping to find a way to get them nominated for the award. I was impressed that she came to me with an ask that wasn't for herself. It was generous and thoughtful, and I remember it.

These examples are what thoughtful, interesting, and inspiring offers and asks look like. They don't have to be big, require a lot of time or effort, or cost anything. They can be authentic and honest and lead to genuine personal relationships. That's how you want to connect.

We need help from other people to succeed in the Gig Economy, so we have to get good at asking for it. We also don't always want to be on the receiving end of help, so we need to learn to make good offers to keep our networks balanced and strong.

The Offer

Offers can vary tremendously, from important introductions and customer or financing leads to smaller overtures like a book recommendation, directions to the best coffee shop in a city someone is traveling to, or a link to a relevant article or talk.

What Is a Good Offer?

A good offer demonstrates that you've already thought carefully about the recipient's situation and have spent some time evaluating how you could support them. A good offer is one that the recipient finds valuable, helpful, and relevant. It's specific, thoughtful, and meets a need or solves a problem of the person receiving it. For example:

Not a good offer: "Let me know if I can do anything to help."

Why this is not a good offer: It is vague, generic, and impersonal and shifts the burden to the recipient to define and articulate what she wants from you.

Chances this offer will be valued: Low

A better offer: "My friend John runs the IT department at Company X. If you'd like, I'll make an introduction so you can introduce your technology product and get his feedback."

Why this is a good offer: It is thoughtful, clear, targeted, and specific and gives a concrete benefit to the recipient.

Chances this offer will be valued: High

Particularly early in their careers, some people get stuck on feeling that they do not have anything to offer or that they are not an expert in anything, but the truth is that everyone has something to offer. Offers of intern-like help such as copyediting an article, researching a fact in question, surfacing an old speech that has been elusive, or referrals to friends that are looking for internships or entry-level positions can all be hugely valuable at the right times. You might not be able to create an offer for everyone, and certainly not right away, but if the connection is important, listen, and over time you'll find a way to help.

The Ask

Your ask is a request to help you to move forward with your current life, projects, or work. Maybe your ask is for job leads, recommendations for consulting work, or introductions, referrals, information, or expertise. Perhaps you need a good vacation recommendation, referrals to a great restaurant in a different city, or perspectives on your next step.

What Is a Good Ask?

For most of us, it's easy to come up with specific ideas about what we need or want. The challenge lies in formulating a good ask that gets us the result we're seeking. A good ask is specific, thoughtful, targeted, and respectful of the demands you are placing on the other person's time, energy, and (if you're requesting introductions or referrals) political or social capital. For example:

Not a good ask: "Are you free to grab coffee or lunch? I'd love to pick your brain."

Why this is not a good ask: It is vague, generic, impersonal, and requests both an undefined amount of time and effort (to meet somewhere other than the individual's office).

Chances this ask will be successful: Low

---

continued on next page

continued from previous page

A better ask: "I just read the series of articles you published on networking. I'd love the chance to ask you about your perspective on inbound connecting and interview you for an article I'm writing on the topic. Are you available sometime in the next three weeks to schedule a 15-minute call to discuss?"

Why this is a good ask: It is thoughtful, clear, targeted, and specific, demonstrates research, respects the person's time, and does not require any effort beyond the 15 minutes requested.

Chances this ask will be successful: High

A good ask takes time to craft and execute. It requires you to do the research and distill what you're seeking into a clear and specific request. The payoff is that a good ask has a much higher chance of being successful and will immediately set you apart from the majority of people who make bad, vague asks.

Asking for Introductions and Referrals

Introductions and referrals are a common ask and the crux of connecting. Yet they're also frequently executed poorly. When you make a request for an introduction, you're asking for the introducer's time and effort and some of her social capital. The right way to ask for an introduction is to be respectful of all three.

I. Respect the Introducer's Time

Similar to the ask described above, be sure to make a specific, targeted request for an introduction.

Not a good ask for an introduction: "I'm seeking opportunities at Company X and would appreciate an introduction to any contacts you have."

A better ask for an introduction: "I'm applying for the manager of business development role at Company X, and I see from your LinkedIn network that you're connected to [John, who works there]. Would you be willing to make an introduction?"

2. Respect the Introducer's Effort

The gold standard for making introductions is the "double opt-in," which means that both parties agree in advance to be introduced. This requires the introducer to first reach out to the person you're asking to meet to confirm that he's willing to take the introduction. If so, then the connection can be made.

To facilitate the double opt-in, provide the introducer with a ready-to-forward email that describes who you are in one to two sentences, includes a link to your LinkedIn profile, and briefly states why you are seeking to speak/meet/interact with the person to whom you're being introduced.

3. Respect the Introducer's Social Capital

Every time we make an introduction, we put our credibility and brand on the line. Too many bad, irrelevant, or off-the-mark introductions will cause people in our network to, at best, stop taking our introductions, and, at worst, question our judgment. When you ask for an introduction, be mindful of the introducer's personal brand and social capital. This means being proactive and responsive in scheduling time to speak or meet with the person to whom you've been introduced, being focused and clear when you do meet, and sending a thank you after you meet. It's also courteous to follow up with introducers to let them know the connection actually took place and what came of it.

In general, people in your network will want to be helpful. Your job when creating asks is to be a person worth helping by being judicious, thoughtful, and specific about your asks.

Maintain Your Network

The final step of connecting is putting a system in place to maintain the good network that you spent time and effort building. The easiest way to do this is to implement some sort of system that will prompt you to connect and track those connections. It could be a simple system of adding reminders to your calendar to connect with specific people. Or keeping a spreadsheet of relationships you want to nurture or deepen and consulting it once a week to track who you've contacted. Implement any system that reminds you to reach out and continue cultivating your connections.

INBOUND AND OUTBOUND CONNECTING
IS THE NEW NETWORKING

Connecting with the right people is critical to succeed in the Gig Economy. Other people are our greatest source of ideas, opportunities, and referrals. We have to generate our own opportunities and plan to change jobs, gigs, and projects frequently in the Gig Economy, so finding ways that we feel comfortable connecting with others is essential to our success.

To build connections without networking, consider:

- ▶ What ways of Inbound and Outbound Connecting are most authentic for me, and what can I do more of?
- ▶ How can I be more thoughtful in the offers and asks that I make of others?
- ▶ What system can I put in place to maintain stronger connections to the network I already have?

Part Two

TAKING *More* TIME OFF

• Chapter Five •

FACE FEAR BY REDUCING RISK

There is only one thing that makes a dream impossible to achieve: the fear of failure.

—PAULO COELHO, *The Alchemist*

Fear can be our biggest and worst enemy. It limits our ability to realize our dreams and keeps us trapped in our everyday lives. The fears that hold us back are big, emotional, and often disconnected from the realities of our actual situation.

Beth is an example of someone who faced unfounded fears about unlikely outcomes when she first considered starting her own business. Beth had been working at a medium-sized firm in leadership development for a decade. She was successful in her job and had built up an excellent portfolio generating revenues for the business and delivering results for clients. But when she started seriously flirting with the idea of starting her own company, she hesitated. Despite all her resources and qualifications, Beth was afraid of failing. Beth is a professor and a sharp businessperson. Those who know her would characterize her as highly intelligent and powerful. And still, there she was, caught up in her fears. As Beth said, "The worst-case scenario is that I'm homeless somewhere with no money."

Why does fear have such a stranglehold on our lives? Why does it hold us back and keep us small even when the opportunity for something bigger and better lies right in front of us? One reason is that we let our fears fester and grow, unchallenged, in our heads. We don't examine them in the cold light of day and see what they're made of. Another reason is that we are loss averse. We feel the pain of loss much more than the pleasure of gain. We pay greater attention to potential losses than gains, and we're inclined to avoid possible setbacks more than we are to seek potential wins.

Facing Fear

It's easiest to deconstruct our fears and identify our risks if we see them in front of us. Let's return to the example of Beth and evaluate her fears of being homeless with no money. Beth had savings and owned a condominium with some equity. At the time, she was single, so her expenses were relatively lean. She was a good candidate for a job in her field, had a strong network of contacts, and had excellent client references. She had an emotionally and financially stable family and a group of local friends.

Beth would have to fall through a lot of safety nets in her life to end up homeless with no money. Life can be harsh, and we could probably construct a scenario in which it could happen, but it would be a highly unlikely one. As Beth noted, for her worst-case scenario to happen, "All my family had to be dead. All my friends had to be dead. There were a whole of things that had to go wrong all together for that outcome to happen." We all have fears like Beth's that, on examination, are more smoke than fire.

Face Fear by Starting with the Worst Case

Our fears are usually big and emotional, and the best way to start facing them is to start with the worst-case scenario. Start with what scares you the most.

Fear

- ▶ I'll be homeless
- ▶ I'll have no money

Once it is written down on paper, it becomes easier to more objectively evaluate it and question: How likely is this to happen? If it's likely, can I live with it? Can I recover from it? Are there actions I can take to prevent this scenario from happening?

Face Fear by Identifying Specific Risks

Once you've named your big, emotional, and vague fears, start to identify the specific, concrete risks that would have to manifest for this worst-case scenario to come true. What often happens in this phase is that you begin to understand the extremely unlikely events that would have to occur for your fear to be realized.

Fear	Risk	Likelihood
I'll be homeless.	I won't be able to afford to pay my mortgage.	Unlikely
	If I sell my condo, I won't be able to rent anywhere.	Highly unlikely
	If I have no home of my own, there is no one I can stay with to get back on my feet.	Highly unlikely
I'll have no money.	I will start my new business and have no revenue.	Possible
	I won't be able to find any clients/customers.	Possible
	If my new business fails, I won't be able to get a job.	Unlikely

Face Fear by Assessing How to Reduce Your Risk

The final step is to develop an action plan to reduce the risks that you can control. You can decide later whether the risks are large or likely enough to warrant taking preventive action, but even having the option to take action can help reduce fear.

The goal of this exercise is to take our big, vague, emotional fears, separate out the concrete risks, and develop a plan of action. Beth's case illustrates that her worst-case fears are unlikely given her situation. That's not uncommon, but sometimes our fears are rooted in likely outcomes. In those cases, this exercise can be very helpful in identifying actions you can take to reduce risks.

It's possible that after completing this exercise, you've come across risks that are too big for your personal risk tolerance, even after you attempt to deal with them. In this case, you may want to consider modifying or restructuring the thing you want to do so that it's smaller and less risky. For example, maybe after completing this exercise you determine that you really aren't in a good financial position to start your own business. If so, can you still move forward with your plan if you start building your business on the side? Starting it as a side gig would help you increase your income, begin to build a client base, and save some money. Or, what if you plan to start your business 12 months from now, to give yourself time to improve your financial condition? During that year, you'll have time to plan, refine your model, earn extra income, save money, and reduce your expenses before starting your business.

This exercise works with any decision you're confronting and with both personal and professional fears. It's an effective way to help you work through decisions like moving cities, changing jobs, getting married, buying a house, and whether or not to go skydiving.

Fear	Risk	Likelihood	Actions
I'll be homeless.	I won't be able to afford to pay my mortgage.	Unlikely	Set aside savings, in a separate account, of a fixed number of months of mortgage payments; take on a part-time job or side gig to increase your income.
	If I sell my condo, I won't be able to rent anywhere.	Highly unlikely	Meet with a realtor and assess the current selling price and costs of downsizing.
	If I have no home of my own, there is no one I can stay with to get back on my feet.	Highly unlikely	Consider subletting the apartment while you move in with friends/parents/a significant other and live for free; consider Airbnb when you travel/are away.
I'll have no money	I will start my new business and have no revenue.	Possible	Start generating revenue through a side gig; secure an anchor client before you make the leap.
	I won't be able to find any clients/ customers.	Possible	Update and connect with your network; have current contact info; be ready to ask for referrals once you make the leap; evaluate if any former or current clients will follow you.
	If my new business fails, I won't be able to get a job.	Unlikely	Stay in touch with recruiters and abreast of changes and movements in your industry; keep in touch with your network; give yourself a fixed amount of time to launch your business or re-enter the job market.

Reducing Risk

The key to facing our fears is breaking them down into their component risks. Risks are concrete and specific, and once we've identified a risk, there are several options for evaluating it and dealing with it. Below are six possible options for dealing with risk. As you break down your fears into their underlying risks, consider each of the options below:

Reduce Risk by Mitigating It

If the risk you're contemplating seems too high for your personal risk tolerance, you might be able to mitigate it. For example, John works full time at an accounting firm whose clients are medium- and large-sized businesses. If John's employer goes out of business, John's income would go from 100 percent to 0. John is uncomfortable with that risk, so he has developed a side business working with entrepreneurs and small businesses, helping them with their bookkeeping, financial statements, and taxes (these clients are not competitive with his employer). The side gig mitigates his worst-case scenario by giving him an income cushion. If he unexpectedly got laid off, his income would go from 100 percent to 30 percent, thanks to his existing client base. If he had a month or two of notice that he was being terminated, he could likely ramp up his side business by actively seeking new clients. He might be able to limit his downside to a reduction of 50 percent of his income. Having the side business allows John to limit his risk of having no income if he gets laid off.

Reduce Risk by Insuring It

If there's an unlikely but terrible outcome that has you worried, see if you can insure it. We insure our risks all the time through health, disability, and home insurance, but there are many other, less-common forms of insurance for specific situations. If you're afraid of taking that once-in-a-lifetime family safari to Africa because you're worried you'll get sick and be unable to get medical care, then look for travel insurance that includes medical evacuation. If you're retiring and planning to sit on some corporate boards of directors, make sure they cover you with directors and officers (D&O) insurance to protect you against lawsuits brought against the company and its directors. If you want to try your hand at working and living on a cargo ship but the thought of Somali pirates keeps you up at night, some kidnapping and ransom (K&R) insurance should calm your fears (and increase your odds of getting out alive).

Reduce Risk by Shifting It

Sometimes you can reduce your risk by shifting some or all of it onto another person or organization. Full-time employees shift the risk of income volatility to their employer because employees get paid a fixed amount every two weeks regardless of the company's actual revenues, profits, or performance. Of course, in the medium term, the company can lay you off or fire you, but in the short term, the risk is higher for the company. Small business owners, in contrast, bear this risk themselves.

In the Gig Economy, we're seeing a big risk shift from companies to workers. Companies are hiring fewer full-time employees. Instead, they hire more contractors, consultants, and on-demand workers, who each take on the risk of volatility in demand for their services and variability in their incomes. Ways to shift economic risk back include signing fixed-price or fixed-length contracts in which your income is guaranteed so long as you fulfill the conditions of the contract, or creating retainer relationships with clients, where they pay you a fixed price in advance each month, for variable work to be specified.

Reduce Risk by Eliminating It

There are some specific situations that allow us to eliminate risks entirely. If you're a contractor or consultant, you can eliminate the risk of not getting paid for a project by negotiating a payment schedule in which you're paid in advance. Contracts are also useful to eliminate risk. If you have an employment contract, you have some comfort that you won't be let go without a specified amount of notice and a fixed amount of severance that you've agreed to and can plan around. Contracts can eliminate the risk and uncertainty around identifiable scenarios by negotiating the outcomes in advance.

Reduce Risk by Accepting It

We regularly accept risk in our lives because most activities involve some degree of risk, even if it's remote. We make reasonable trade-offs about the size of the risk and the probability that it will occur compared to the rewards we expect from pursuing the activity. How much risk we're willing to accept depends on our personal risk tolerance. Heli skiers and skydivers are willing to accept relatively higher levels of risk for the thrill of pursuing those activities. Most of us are willing to accept low levels of risk in our daily lives. We eat out in restaurants, even though there's a chance of food poisoning. We go swimming, even though we could drown, and we take buses and trains that have some small chance of crashing.

Be aware that our levels of risk seeking and risk aversion can vary by situation. I might enjoy racecar driving but be averse to investing in the stock market. I can be both risk seeking in some areas and risk averse in others, so the levels of risk I'm willing to accept can vary as well.

EXERCISE

Face Your Fears and
Reduce Your Risks

STEP 1: START WITH THE WORST CASE

Imagine the most negative outcome of the decision you're most afraid of, the extreme consequences, and the most frightening results. Write them down.

STEP 2: IDENTIFY SPECIFIC RISKS

Identify specific, concrete risks that make up your fears. List as many as you can think of.

STEP 3: ASSESS HOW TO REDUCE YOUR RISK

Develop an action plan for each risk. Go through each risk and evaluate: Can I mitigate it, insure it, shift it, eliminate it, or accept it? Determine the risk of taking no action.

Complete steps 1 through 3 on your own, and then walk through the exercise with someone else. It's most useful to work through the exercise with someone who can help you look more objectively at your fears and risks. Ideally you would complete this exercise with someone who has already been through or experienced the thing that you're contemplating, Someone who has been there, done that, will be in the best position to draw on her own experiences to help you break down your fears and make a plan to reduce your risks.

Consider the Risk of a Boring Life

There are risks associated with every action. But equally important to consider are the risks of inaction. It's important to ask ourselves: What is the risk of not taking enough risk? What is the risk of living too comfortable, too secure, too stable a life? What if we play it too safe and fail to grow, fail to thrive, fail to even try to pursue our dreams? Which is more frightening to contemplate: the risk of failure or the risk of regret? The risk of a loud crash and fall, or the life of quiet desperation?

Amber Rae is a blogger, artist, and entrepreneur who encourages us to take risk, "to invent new careers, act on ideas and create a life that drives [us] forward." She humorously summarizes the risks of a life of inaction in a fake book title: *Be Mediocre: The Ultimate Guide to Climbing the Corporate Ladder, Asking for Permission, and Living a Boring Life.*[1] There is such a thing as living a life that is too safe.

What would you want the book about your life to be titled?

See Your Blind Spot

As you work through the previous exercise, it can help to do some research and data gathering about the probability and likelihood of various risks. Having facts and figures to quantify some of the risks will give you the information to accurately assess their probability. That information alone could help reduce your fears. For example, Beth might have in mind that over 75 percent of small businesses fail, and that probability contributes to her fear of starting her own business. But if she researched that assumption, she might find that (for example) 90 percent of restaurants fail after a year and 80 percent of retail establishments go out of business but only 30 percent of professional services firms fail in the first year. Just having better information can help Beth overcome some of her fear.

We're not very good at assessing our fears and risks accurately. Our assessment of risk is distorted by a series of cognitive biases like overconfidence (which researchers implicate in gambling), anchoring (we assess gains and losses depending on how they are framed), and loss aversion (we hate losses more than we love equivalent gains). These cognitive biases can cause us to either overestimate or underestimate risk and make (sometimes big) decisions based on our inaccurate perception.

We tend to hold unfounded fears about events and outcomes that are unlikely yet seem oblivious to the very real risks in our everyday lives. Driving is an excellent example of our inability to accurately assess risk. Automobile accidents are the leading cause of death for teenagers and one of the top 10 causes of death in the United States. Cars are the third most dangerous mode of vehicle transport (behind motorcycles and bikes). An average 20- to 30-minute commute by car each way has been associated with increased obesity, depression, anxiety, and social isolation. Yet few Americans would identify daily driving as one of the riskiest activities they pursue, even if the data is clear about the dangers. Every day we fearlessly take significant risks. This means that we probably have more risk in our lives than we would comfortably take on if we could see it clearly.

Our evaluation of risk is also influenced by emotions and personal experiences. Many of my MBA students who watched their parents get laid off or downsized after several decades at a company believe that working for themselves or starting their own business provides more job security and is lower risk than a corporate job. Yet there are just as many students who grew up in an entrepreneurial household who believe exactly the opposite: that self-employment and startup life is risky and financially volatile and that the safe, fiscally conservative choice is to get a traditional job.

When we don't assess risks accurately, we can end up taking high risks (driving our car to the grocery store) for low rewards (food shopping). We take on too much risk because we experience too little fear. Or, even worse, we miss out on potentially high rewards (fulfillment, contentment, happiness, wonderful memories) because we mistakenly avoid activities that seem high risk (quitting a bad job, taking that family safari, having that third kid). We take on too little risk because we have too much fear. In both cases, our inability or unwillingness to accurately assess the fears and risks we're facing causes us to make suboptimal, or even inappropriate, decisions. By breaking down and analyzing our risks and gathering information, we can be more accurate and explicit about which risks are worth taking.

Learn to Be a Better Risk Taker

Some risk taking in our lives is necessary, healthy, and required for growth. While we should make every effort to avoid destructive risk taking—like smoking or driving drunk—positive risk taking is necessary to progress in our lives. Moving out of our parents' house, starting a new job, accepting a promotion, making a new friend, learning a new skill, or relocating to a different city can all help us grow, gain confidence, and open up new opportunities. Positive risks expose us to the possibility of failure, but without taking those risks, we won't grow. There are ways we can learn and practice to be better risk takers.

Take Small Risks

Take baby steps. Start small. Increase your risk tolerance by taking smaller risks first, and then slowly increase to taking larger risks as you feel comfortable. If taking a year off seems too risky to you, start with just a month off. If you're afraid to move across country, start by visiting for a few weeks or agreeing to spend a month in the West Coast office to try it out. In their research on risk, Norris Krueger Jr. and Peter Dickson of Ohio State University found that engaging in small doses of risk-taking behavior is an effective way to increase our confidence, which, in turn, increases our risk taking.[2]

Take Safe Risks

Adopt a framework of taking safe risks that have limited downsides. Getting a new haircut is an example of a safe risk because the downside is limited to looking a little less fabulous during the time it takes your hair to grow back. In the Gig Economy, part-time side gigs can offer a way to take a safe risk. If quitting your job and working for yourself seems too risky, a part-time side gig offers the potential to learn more about the opportunity before you commit fully and test if you can generate revenue and get customers. If it doesn't work out or you hate it, you lose the time, energy, and cash you allocated to invest in the gig, but you've avoided the bigger loss of your job.

Expect and Prepare to Fail

Researchers at New York University found that giving ourselves permission to fail can make us better risk takers.[3] Participants in their study were told to pretend that the gambling task they were given was something they performed every day and that losses were not only acceptable but to be expected. Those participants outperformed their peers who weren't given those instructions. The students that were given permission to fail took smart risks, and they worried less when they were told to expect losses. The researchers concluded that good risk taking can be taught by helping students to build up a tolerance for risk.

We can see this effect in the entrepreneurial ecosystem or in places with high levels of entrepreneurial activity and a risk-taking culture, like San Francisco and Boston. When failure is expected and culturally accepted, people become more comfortable, more frequent, and better risk takers.

Plan for the Best-Case Scenario

Sometimes we spend so much time focused on the downside (our fear rearing its ugly head) that we don't spend enough time contemplating the upside. Of course it's prudent to have a financial cushion and a plan if your new business fails. But what if it wildly succeeds? Are you prepared for that? Do you have a short list of the team members you'd like to hire, the financing you'd need to get, the high-profile customers you'd target?

Once you've gone through this fear and risk exercise and made your action plan, turn your attention to how you'll handle success. What's your best-case scenario? How likely is it to happen? What factors could cause it to happen? How would you need to react in the short and medium term? What resources would you need? Spend time imagining your success. Hopefully that's the action plan you'll need.

FACING FEAR AND REDUCING RISK IS
THE NEW COMFORT ZONE

The Gig Economy offers plenty of opportunity and potential rewards but also higher risks. There is more job insecurity, income variability, and change in the Gig Economy.

To make sure that we don't let fear keep us from pursuing a career or life that could bring us the highest rewards, consider:

- ▶ What are my fears and the worst-case scenarios I worry about?
- ▶ Have I identified, evaluated, and developed an action plan to reduce the risks associated with my fears?
- ▶ How can I practice and learn to be a better risk taker?
- ▶ Have I planned for the best-case scenario?

• Chapter Six •

TAKE TIME OFF BETWEEN GIGS

I had never been happy with the bourgeois virtues of
marriage, stability, and work above pleasure. I was too
curious and adventurous not to chafe under those
restrictions.

—ERICA JONG, *Fear of Flying*

My fiancé (now husband) and I were boarding a plane to Tokyo,
the first stop on our round-the-world ticket. We had quit our
corporate jobs, sold our car, and ended the lease on our apartment. We stuffed our two big backpacks and left our few remaining possessions stored in the garage of my childhood home.
We were taking a year off to travel around the world, a dream
we had been talking about since we met in college and had been
planning for nearly a year. Our itinerary included four months
in Asia, some time in Africa, and almost two months in Austra-
lia—all places that are hard to visit during a standard corporate
two-week vacation.

Colleagues and friends reacted to the news of our trip with
mixed emotions that ranged from enthusiasm and support, to
envy, to warnings that we were foolish to quit our good jobs
and damage our careers. We listened, but we were committed
to our plan and convinced that we didn't want to wait until
"someday . . ." to travel. We wanted to go when we were young,

fit, and still willing to backpack. Being in the honeymoon phase of our relationship was also a plus. So we went ahead and had an incredible year of travel, learning, experiences, and time together. Looking back, I consider that year one of my biggest and most meaningful accomplishments.

The Gig Economy requires us to think about time off differently. Instead of being granted two to three weeks of annual paid vacation from our job, we can expect to have more frequent and regular periods of time off throughout our working lives as a result of normal lulls between gigs and between jobs. We also have more freedom and flexibility to take more time off because we exert greater control over where, when, and how much we work.

The question to answer is: What do I want to do with that time?

Developing Ideas for Time Off

The chance to take more time off presents us with enormous opportunities to live a more varied, interesting, and balanced life. Instead of squeezing our personal goals and dreams into a two-week vacation each year, we can take time between gigs and between jobs to pursue them. In the Gig Economy, it's easier to take more time off more frequently. We can plan ahead to be "job free" and pursue other life goals, such as writing that novel, traveling, spending time with our children or aging parents, volunteering, or whatever else is on our bucket list. If we use it intentionally, time off between gigs can be some of the most satisfying and meaningful in our lives.

During my interviews for this book, I asked people both in the Gig Economy and in traditional corporate jobs how they would most want to spend time between gigs. Several common themes emerged. These broad themes can be a starting point to spark your own ideas and specific plans for the next time you're between gigs.

Travel: Travel tops the list of responses every time. Sometimes it's travel for travel's sake: taking a vacation, visiting a particular country or part of the world, or taking that backpacking trip that never happened in college. It's equally often about travel with a purpose: visiting the town in Italy where the family is from, going on a trip with dad to see every baseball stadium, spending a few weeks with grandparents, or visiting college friends who are spread out across the country.

Pursue an interest or passion: The second most popular response is to spend more time pursuing activities and interests, such as improving a golf game, training for a marathon or triathlon, or even just creating a routine to exercise regularly. Others want to devote time to a favorite hobby, like gardening, reading, painting, or photography. Many people I interviewed would use the time to pursue an activity or passion, but with a specific goal in mind: to learn a new language, become a certified yoga teacher, get qualified to teach English as a second language, or become a better cook.

Volunteer: Giving back was a common desire, but the ways to do so varied tremendously: join a political campaign, build houses for Habitat for Humanity, help provide free healthcare through Remote Area Medical, maintain the Appalachian trail, help on an organic farm, or donate time to a charity.[1] There are so many opportunities to volunteer that it's easy to identify one that overlaps with almost any area of interest.

Complete personal projects: This category includes things like completing all those projects we've been meaning to start: organizing our photos, cleaning out the garage, putting our finances in order, or experiencing *The Life-Changing Magic of Tidying Up.*[2] Or maybe your personal project is taking some personal time: spiritual activities such as meditation or yoga retreats or whatever else nourishes, calms, and rejuvenates you.

We want to be intentional about our time off and, like Goldilocks, structure it just the right amount—not too much and not too little. If we overstructure, it can limit the free time and space we need to rejuvenate and we can lose the spontaneity and serendipity that leads us to new adventures. But if we understructure, we might never get off the couch. Consider what works for you, and pick the amount of structure that is just right.

It can take some practice to get used to intentionally structuring time off. It's not a skill that full-time employees have needed to develop, so it can take a few tries to get both good and comfortable at it. Having a list of ideas at the ready helps. It keeps us from falling into the trap of wasting or frittering away time off that we could use more intentionally to realize our dreams, advance our goals, and honor our priorities.

EXERCISE

Taking a Year Off

Everyone has a different list of priorities and goals or long-held dreams that they want to realize. The key to taking more time off is to expect it, plan for it, and have a pipeline of ideas about what you want to do with it. The purpose of this exercise is to encourage you to dream big about what you would do with more time off, without the normal constraints of time and money. It's designed to help you move away from a resource-based conversation and create a wide, unconstrained mental space to explore and imagine possibilities.

OPTION 1: IMAGINE A YEAR OFF

Imagine if next year you were given one year off and one year's salary. Write down your answers to the following question: What would I do with that time and those resources?

Sometimes it can be hard to imagine structuring that much free time, particularly if you've been an employee for a while and aren't used to having control over your time. If that's the case for you, start with option 2, which is a smaller version of the previous exercise.

OPTION 2: IMAGINE A SUMMER OFF

Imagine if next year you were given three months off and one quarter (25 percent) of your salary. Write down your answers to the following question: What would I do with that time and those resources?

The idea of this exercise is to start exploring and listing ideas that can be implemented during shorter periods of time off. We don't have to take off a lot of time for it to be significant. Even short periods of time, if planned for, can be meaningful.

This exercise is most effective if you complete it first by yourself and then discuss and brainstorm your answers with a like-minded significant other, family member, or close friend. That person might contribute other interesting ideas you hadn't considered or be so inspired that he or she offers to join you!

It's easiest and most effective to always be planning for time off and make this exercise an ongoing one. Keep a running list of ideas, big and small, that you'd like to pursue in your additional time. These ideas don't have to cost anything or involve grand plans. In fact, make it a point to include ideas that would fit into a few days or a week of an unexpected work gap: ideas like taking grandma to lunch for the afternoon or to the beach for a day, offering to take mom's car for an oil change while she's at work, sitting on the couch and reading a book for a day, or taking a weekend to watch the Harry Potter series from beginning to end.

If you create a place to note ideas when you think of them, you'll always have a list ready when an unexpected window of time opens. I keep Stickies (digital Post-it notes) on my desktop and have one called "Time Off" that I use to note ideas about projects and possibilities I'd like to pursue when I next have time between gigs. A friend of mine carries around a small notebook and jots down lists of books he wants to read, concepts for personal projects, and business ideas he wants to spend time exploring. The exact method doesn't matter. It's the process of tracking our interests, ideas, and dreams that's important. Once you have identified and written down your own ideas and dreams, you can plan—even if it's one, two, or five years ahead—to do the things you most want to do.

Financing Time Off

Ask anyone why they don't take more time off, and the most common response will be that they don't have the money to do so. This is a valid concern and in some cases an insurmountable obstacle. But often it's simply an excuse that keeps us nestled deep inside in our comfort zone. With planning, and a willingness to make trade-offs, most of us can finance some version of our vision of time off. A year flying around on a culinary tour of Europe next month might be out of reach, but a month with a Eurorail pass and a backpack a year from now could be possible. Creativity, planning, and time can go a long way to making our visions a reality.

Chapter 8 covers financial issues in the Gig Economy in more detail, but following are some ideas that are specific to financing time off between gigs.

Get laid off: Getting laid off from a full-time professional job almost always involves a lump-sum payout of some kind from severance, unused vacation, or a prorated bonus. It also usually means you qualify for unemployment. Allocate some (not all!) of your severance cash to finance taking time off before you start your next gig.

Negotiate start and end dates: The least-stressful way to start taking time off is when you have your next gig lined up and you know when your next paycheck is arriving. It's a low-cost and low-risk way to get comfortable taking blocks of time off.

Jason is a good example of someone who started taking time off by negotiating his start date. He was getting ready to leave his full-time job in June and move himself and his family to another city for his new job. He was finishing work at his old firm on Friday and intended to start his new job on Monday. We happened to talk before that plan was finalized, and I encouraged him to negotiate a much later September start date. A start date after Labor Day would give him the summer off with his three kids and time to relocate and settle into his new city. He admitted he hadn't thought of, let along considered, that option but liked the idea. As he and his new employer finalized the details of his new role, Jason put out the idea of a fall start date. Starting in September meant that he would miss a key senior leadership retreat, which his new boss wanted him to attend, so they agreed on a mid-August start date instead. Just by asking, Jason secured two months of time off, from mid-June until mid-August. He was able to spend the summer with his family and help get everyone settled in their new home and new city before he started his new job. The best part was that it was a very relaxing period of time off because he knew the exact date he'd start getting paid again.

Pick a longer time horizon: If taking time off right now is unaffordable, try extending the time horizon to plan to take time off in a year or two years. With planning, we have time to work more and/or spend less to save for what we most want to do.

Practice taking small amounts of time off: The time off we take doesn't have to be long and expensive to be meaningful. Start by practicing the habit of taking small periods of time off that don't require significant financial resources. Begin by planning for and taking just a week or two in between gigs or building in a few days at the end of each consulting project. Try using the time in different ways—volunteering, catching up with friends or family, or relaxing and rejuvenating—and see what feels good. Use these small and inexpensive blocks of time to experiment.

Go away: Consider taking time off in a lower-cost location. Spending the summer living in Asia and working on your novel could be much cheaper than writing it in Paris or New York City. A month of volunteering in Iowa or Appalachia will be cheaper than working for a nonprofit organization in San Francisco. Home swapping, renting, or Airbnb-ing your home can help reduce your accommodation costs even

further. Depending on the costs of getting to and from another location, heading to a cheaper part of the country or the
world can meaningfully cut the costs of time off.

What Will the Neighbors (and Your Friends and Family) Think?

The Gig Economy is not a brand new phenomenon, but it's still
new to many people. Your parents or grandparents, your boss, or
the person interviewing you at a large corporation may not fully
understand or grasp the changeable nature of work in the Gig
Economy. They may be entrenched in an Employee Mindset
that makes it hard to follow and understand your decision to
take time off. They might not understand what you're doing or
why, and they could be concerned about your financial and professional progress.

When we take time off, we need a story to tell our family,
friends, and colleagues that explains what we're doing and
places it in the context of our goals and priorities. We want a
coherent and compelling narrative that helps them understand
why we're taking time off. We want to make sure that we don't
appear undirected, or slacking off, because we're taking some
time away from working. Our goal is to make it easy for our
friends and family to support us by communicating what we're
doing and why.

There will always be at least some people who begrudge our
willingness and ability to take time off. When we pursue an
alternative path, it can be hugely threatening to people who have
chosen a more traditional course by default. We can end up being on the receiving end of someone else's envy, jealousy, and
resentment. The most we can do for this audience is explain the
intentional planning, the focus on our priorities, and the

trade-offs we made to be able to take time off and encourage them to do the same if it's something they'd actually like to do.

We must also be sensitive when we deal with older generations of parents and grandparents or older colleagues, as they can still be very rooted in an Employee Mindset where time off consists of receiving two weeks of annual vacation. We have to help them realize that we're not "given" annual vacation if we're not currently working a full-time job. We now have to plan for and "take" our own time. Our goal is to help them understand the value of how we're using our time and how it aligns with our life goals and personal priorities.

It can help us tell our own story if we refer to the stories of others. Successful role models can serve as examples of how time off can be a useful, productive, and rejuvenating break. Stefan Sagmeister is a designer who runs his own studio in New York City. In his popular TED talk The Power of Time Off, he advocates his approach of taking regular intervals of time off during his working life.[3] He presents a tantalizing suggestion:

> We spend about 25 years of our lives learning. Then there is about 40 years that's really reserved for working. And then, tacked on at the end of it, are about 15 years of retirement. And I thought it might be helpful to basically cut off five of those retirement years and intersperse them in between those working years.

Every seven years, Stefan takes a one-year sabbatical and closes his studio during that time. He has found that his time off is successful both creatively and financially; the work he produces after his sabbatical is higher quality, and he is able to charge more for it.

Anne-Marie Slaughter, author, professor at Princeton University, and president and CEO of the think tank New America, coined the term "investment interval" to describe the time off she took to spend 10 months living abroad with her family.

> My husband and I took a sabbatical in Shanghai, from August 2007 to May 2008, right in the thick of an election year when many of my friends were advising various candidates on foreign-policy issues. We thought of the move in part as "putting money in the family bank," taking advantage of the opportunity to spend a close year together in a foreign culture. But we were also investing in our children's ability to learn Mandarin and in our own knowledge of Asia.[4]

Both Bill Bryson and Cheryl Strayed have written books about their time off immersing in nature and paring their lives down to what they could carry in a backpack.[5]

There are many more examples of people of all ages, professions, and economic circumstances who have taken time off in all sorts of ways and successfully transitioned back into the workforce. I could fill the rest of this book with examples, but a simple search for year-off blogs will yield pages of results that give a sense of the creative ways people spend their time off. Having these examples and role models can help us create our own stories that will help the people we care about support us more and worry less.

Mind the Gap (on Your Resume)

Examples of time off that will resonate more with your colleagues in the corporate world can be found by talking to employees of some of *Fortune*'s list of the 100 Best Companies to Work For. Nearly one quarter of companies on the list offer paid sabbaticals to employees, including Boston Consulting Group, PricewaterhouseCoopers, and General Mills.[6] The sabbaticals that employees take range in duration and focus. Employees I interviewed for this book spent their paid sabbaticals traveling to Ireland with their kids during summer vacation, living in an apartment in Paris for a month, backcountry hiking and camping for a week, and taking a "staycation" to renovate their home.

Many corporations don't offer sabbaticals, so it can be a daunting task to explain time off to colleagues or as part of a job interview. Some periods of time off might be too small to show up in a meaningful way on your resume, but for longer periods of time, it's a good idea to have a story ready about how you made productive and meaningful use of the time off. Being able to tell an engaging and interesting story about your time off can alter people's perspectives about it and let them know you weren't on the couch binge-watching Netflix (well, at least not all the time!).

Devin is a great example of someone who developed a compelling story about his time off. He had spent nearly a decade working for or with the city of Boston in various economic development roles before being laid off from his job. He wasn't sure what he wanted to do next and was actively job hunting when he decided to take his savings and head off on a road trip across the United States, visiting friends along the way. "I had always wanted to do a cross-country road trip, so I just decided I was going to do it. And on that day I looked up a bunch of different friends I had in different cities, and started to map out a route." Devin spent a month traveling across the United States, visiting friends. Besides talking about realizing a long-held dream, when asked about his time off, Devin says:

> I really care about cities, which is why I worked for the city of Boston and did economic development for them for 8 years. And so for me to go across the country to see 15 different cities, and see what my friends were doing in those cities, was

valuable. It's a thing that I can draw from. I can bring it to work and I can bring it to whatever other jobs I have.

By talking about accomplishing a long-held dream, and connecting elements of his trip to his work, Devin has created a compelling story, both personally and professionally.

Another option is to incorporate some professional activities into your time off. Attend a conference, write some professional articles or a guest blog post, volunteer or offer your services pro bono, or even take a "Jobbatical." Coined by the founders of the eponymous website (jobbatical.com), the site posts short-term job opportunities—anywhere from one to twelve months—from around the world. For those who don't mind combining work and travel, it offers a way to do both.

You can also let your time off tell its own story. Write a blog about what you're doing and learning and thinking, document your 100-days-of-time-off happiness on Instagram, or use Shutterfly and compile your best photographs into a photobook that you can foist on unsuspecting colleagues. Having something you can share helps you stay in touch with your colleagues and friends and gives people a vivid sense of the impressive ways you used your time.

No One Else Takes Time Off: Why Should I?

It's somewhat strange to be in the position of advocating for more time off given the fairly obvious arguments in favor of it: It's fun, relaxing, and good for our health, can reduce stress, and is generally beneficial to the people who take it.[7] Yet apparently the case needs to be made because close to half of Americans (41 percent) don't take even the limited paid time off that we're given, let alone any kind of extended time.[8] The reasons why are primarily in our heads, not at our jobs. Employees are afraid to take time off mostly because they fear returning to a big pile of work or they believe that no one else can do their job while they're gone.[9]

The benefits of time off are much more tangible and plentiful.

Take Time Off to Regain Balance

Many of today's retirees are part of a generation that tended to overconcentrate on work. During their productive years, they concentrated on a limited number of activities: work, family, maybe their lawn. Two weeks of paid time off from their jobs didn't offer much time to learn, grow, explore the world, develop interests and hobbies, or deeply invest in friends or community. As a result, retirees today watch an average of 50 hours of TV per week, according to Nielsen.[10]

We can avoid the mistakes of previous generations and use time between gigs to diversify and expand our personal lives. We can explore our interests, practice being a beginner, develop new hobbies, and meet new people. We can take time to invest in our family or community or in a cause or organization we care about. We can find a better balance.

Let's take the example of Yoon, who was laid off when the nonprofit she was leading shut down. She was mentally and emotionally exhausted from the past four years of working at full speed. She recalls, "I really poured my heart and soul and every physical ounce of my energy into it. So by the time we actually closed it, I was completely exhausted." After such an intense period completely focused on work, she decided to spend two weeks visiting her family overseas, spending time with her many relatives, and deeply relaxing. Once she arrived, "I just took that time to really recover and spend time doing simple things, reading, watching Netflix, appreciating time with my family." Those two weeks at home turned into three months as she realized how much she needed to rebalance and devote some time to herself. When Yoon finally did return to the United States, she realized that "I wanted to give more time to things that are really important to me, not to my career, because I'm burnt by my career." So she took an additional month and went on a spiritual retreat to explore her faith. This intensely personal period with family and on a retreat gave Yoon a way to rebalance and regroup after dedicating so much attention and energy to work.

Take Time Off to Refresh and Rejuvenate

Work can be stressful. Many American workers suffer from not only chronic stress but also short-term and long-term fatigue. In an interview with *Entrepreneur Magazine*, Allison Gabriel, an assistant professor of management at Virginia Commonwealth University, says:

> There is a lot of research that says we have a limited pool of cognitive resources. When you are constantly draining your resources, you are not being as productive as you can be. If you get depleted, we see performance decline. You're able to persist less and have trouble solving tasks.[11]

Taking time off beyond the length of a two-week vacation can help rejuvenate us and replenish our depleted cognitive and emotional resources.

Companies that offer paid sabbaticals to employees do so primarily to give them the chance to refresh and rejuvenate. The Intel Corporation offers its employees eight weeks of paid leave after seven years of employment because employees return "renewed and ready to innovate."[12] Even a relatively short period of time off combined with a digital Sabbath can break the "always on" cycle and allow us to mentally rejuvenate.

Take Time Off to Change Perspective

If you plan time off to include a radical change in your lifestyle or a push outside your comfort zone, it can change your whole perspective on life, even after you return. After three years of planning, Winston Chen quit his job at a software company and moved with his wife and two young children to a Norwegian island for a year to do something "completely different."[13] In a blog post that he wrote about his experience, he summarized the newfound feelings of confidence and peace he felt after returning to the States: "My wife and I said, 'What's the worst that can happen? We go back and live on the island?' We were clothed with the armor of confidence forged from the newfound knowledge that our family could be very happy living on very little." The time away had changed his perspective on his life, his work, and what it took for his family to thrive and be happy. He realized that his time off "wasn't just a memorable adventure. It had made us different people." We don't all have to move to a remote Nordic island to obtain a new perspective. Time off to implement a different routine or pursue new activities can also be powerful ways to change our views of ourselves and our lives.

Take Time Off to Create "In-Between Space"

Our work and home lives can quickly devolve into an all-work, no-play cycle of schedules, busyness, and obligations. We feel rushed, pressured, stressed, and always juggling. There is no yin to our yang. Author and speaker Nilofer Merchant writes about the importance of "in-between space" in our lives; those gaps of time between ending one thing and beginning another:

We've all had in between spaces. Summers when you were young were the in between spaces of learning—where you could languish in play time and know learning time was ahead. It is that time between conceiving your child, and becoming parents when (if you are lucky) you get to antic-ipate the joy but experience none of the hardship. It is the time between an engagement and the wedding. Even on the flip side . . . After a divorce as you learn to find your own voice again. That time where you got a job offer but hadn't started yet. Maybe even during the search for a new role. Perhaps it is as simple as when you are clear of a new direction. In between times are full. Of hope, certainly. Especially, of possibility.[14]

The Gig Economy offers us many opportunities to create, sa-vor, and enjoy pockets of time and space in our lives. Whenever you're transitioning—changing jobs or beginning a new gig, moving cities, or graduating—look for opportunities to cultivate your own "in-between space."

TIME BETWEEN GIGS IS
THE NEW PAID TIME OFF

We have more control of our time, and our time off, in the Gig Economy. Instead of being "given" two weeks of annual paid time off, it's increasingly up to us to "take" time off and decide how to use it. As we go from gig to gig, job to job, and project to project, natural breaks, downtime, and lulls will inevitably occur. These interludes are space and time to pause, to breathe and reflect, and to pursue and chase our dreams.

Taking more time off is a skill. If you want to get good at it, consider:

- How can I anticipate, save, and plan for more time off in the Gig Economy?
- Where can I keep a running list of ideas for how to use my time off in a way that is intentional, meaningful to me, and aligned with my priorities?
- Do I do a good job communicating why and what I'd do/ am doing with time off?

Chapter Seven

BE MINDFUL ABOUT TIME

I'm happy to be reminded that an ordinary day full of nothing but nothingness can make you feel like you've won the lottery.
—SUSAN ORLEAN

Emily realized that she needed to think about her time differently when she transitioned from her job as a full-time teacher to working multiple gigs in book publishing. As a full-time teacher, she was used to selling her entire day to her employer and believed that a hardworking and "good" employee worked on-site at least 8 a.m. to 6 p.m. When Emily left teaching, she started working several part-time gigs as a research assistant and book publicist. She suddenly had some flexibility to structure her own hours during the workday because what mattered most was that she delivered high-quality work, not that she was physically in a school or an office for a fixed number of hours.

It took her a while to break from the 8 a.m. to 6 p.m. mentality. She said, "I had trouble recognizing or accepting that my time was my own. I was in the habit of giving someone else control over my time, and being fully available to them." But eventually she started noticing when she did her best work and when she needed to break. She started adopting a schedule of morning work, followed by lunch and exercise, and then several more hours of mid- to late-afternoon work before stopping in time to enjoy cooking and eating dinner with her boyfriend. She was even able to keep one late afternoon a week to herself to pursue working with a nonprofit. As she got used to owning, then structuring, her time, she felt that she was able to be more efficient and productive, and produce higher quality work. She enjoyed work more, and she feels healthier and happier.

The Gig Economy offers us the chance to structure and control our time in ways that we never could as full-time employees. Working as a contractor can give us unprecedented autonomy to decide where, when, and how much we want to work. Even if we end up working more hours in the Gig Economy, we retain more agency, ownership, and control over where and when those hours occur. These changes encourage us to think explicitly about our time as a resource and be more intentional about how we allocate and structure it. It also gives us more opportunity to align our time with our priorities.

Traditional employees sell their physical presence, mental attention, and intellectual energy for 40+ hours a week, every week, in the office, on the company's schedule. If they finish their work at 3 p.m., they stay until 5 or 6 p.m. and figure out something else to do.

In the Gig Economy, we still sell our time to employers or clients, but not always in big 40-hour-workweek blocks and not under the same terms. If we sell our time, it might only be for a few days or part of a workweek. We're also more likely to sell our results, insights, or impact *instead of* a fixed amount of time. This is an enormous shift in how we think about work and about time. As consultants and contractors, we sell our ability to efficiently and effectively deliver specific outcomes, not our willingness to sit in an office for eight hours every day.

There's some evidence that having control over our work time is becoming more valuable. The Society for Human Resource Management found in a survey of HR professionals that over 70% of companies offered some type of flexible work arrangement that gave employees more control over how many hours, when, or where they worked.[1] About two thirds (65 percent) of the organizations said that employee requests for such arrangements were increasing. A recent survey by Ernst & Young found that work flexibility is an important attribute, second only to competitive pay that Millennials seek when evaluating a job.[2] They also found that not being able to work flexibly is one of the top five reasons they quit their jobs.

Where Does My Time Go?

Author L. R. W. Lee noted that "between the calendar and the checkbook, one's priorities are laid bare." We can talk all we want about what's important to us and what we value, but our true priorities are revealed in how we spend our time and our money (spoiler alert for the Financing the Life You Want section!). To understand how intentional we are with our time, and how well aligned it is with our priorities, it's helpful to take L. R. W. Lee's words to heart and conduct a calendar diagnostic to determine what our priorities have been.

Calendar Diagnostic

STEP 1

Think back to the chapter on success and priorities, and recall the responses to the key questions:

- What does success look like to me?
- What are the values and priorities I want to live?
- What is my definition of a good job, a good career, and even a good life?

STEP 2

Open (or go get) your personal or family calendar and review the past year. Answer the following questions:

- What were my three biggest time commitments each month and each week?
- What did I spend my time doing?
- What did I do on my weekends?
- Did I take any vacations or time off?

STEP 3

Reflect on and answer:

- How much alignment is there between my priorities and how I spent my time?

Be concrete in your answer. If a top priority for you is your health, how many days did you exercise? Bike to work? Go to the gym or a yoga class? Cook at home? For each of your top three priorities, evaluate the alignment between them and your calendar.

It's likely that your calendar diagnostic reveals some misalignment between your priorities and how you spend your time. It's not uncommon because we have several cognitive biases or errors in thinking that can interfere with our ability to make good decisions about how best to use our time. As you read through the list that follows, consider: Which of these biases apply to me?

Do You Feel Bad About Wasting Time?

We're much more likely to waste our time than our money because we have a higher level of pain over losing money than over "losing" or wasting time. For example, tossing a fifty-dollar bill into the fireplace to burn causes us pain over the loss of the fifty dollars, but if we waste an hour in front of that same fire watching cat videos on Facebook, we don't feel the same level of pain.

It doesn't make sense that we feel less loss aversion to wasting time than money because, unlike money, our time here on Earth is so limited. Except for a few tweaks around the edges, like wearing our seatbelts, not smoking, and taking other life-prolonging steps, there's not much we can do to create more of it. We can't bank our time and save it for use later like we can our money. The fixed nature of time would seem to require us to treat it even more carefully and with even more intention than money, but often we don't.

If we want to limit the time we fritter away on things that aren't priorities to us, we need to develop ways to make wasting time feel more painful. We can do this explicitly by creating concrete choices, changing our language, and tracking our time.

Create choice: We can ask ourselves things like: "Do I want to watch cat videos for an hour or read the latest issue of *The New Yorker*?" By forcing ourselves to choose between two concrete options, we increase our awareness of when we're wasting or misallocating our time.

Change our language: Laura Vanderkam, author of the book *168 Hours*, suggests that we change the language we use to talk about our time decisions:

> Instead of saying "I don't have time" try saying "it's not a priority," and see how that feels. I have time to iron my sheets, but I just don't want to. Changing our language reminds us that time is a choice. If we don't like how we're spending an hour, we can choose differently.[3]

Track time: We can track our time usage through technology and pinpoint where we're wasting time and need to make changes. Fitbit can measure the time we spend exercising and sleeping, RescueTime can monitor how we use our screen time, and Moment can tell us how much time we spend on our phones. The ability to quantify ourselves makes it easier than ever to track our daily time habits and identify the ones we want to change.

Do You Allocate Enough Time to Larger, Longer-Term Rewards?

Short-term wins are compelling because they offer instant gratification and a sense of accomplishment and progress. We discussed this tendency briefly in chapter 1 and used the Clayton Christensen "How Will You Measure Your Life?" article to illustrate it. In that article, Christensen's classmates fell prey to this short-term bias by persistently overinvesting in immediate career "wins" and achievements at the expense of the longer-term reward of lasting and loving family relationships. This is a misallocation of time if we're striving to build a meaningful and happy life, since relationships, not our careers, are what deliver those rewards.

This cognitive bias is called *hyperbolic discounting*. Christensen asserts that we need to resist the allure of shorter-term gratification and make an explicit effort to keep our longer-term priorities "front and center" so that we allocate sufficient time and energy toward them. Like the exercises you did previously in chapter 1, explicitly identifying our priorities and values and reminding ourselves of them can be an effective way to overcome this bias.

Do You Know How Much Time Your Stuff Costs You?

We also have a less-rigorous model of mental accounting for time than money, which means that we don't track time investments as closely as investments of money. We keep a closer eye on our checkbook than our calendar. For instance, if we make $75,000 per year, after subtracting 30 percent for taxes, etc., let's say for ease of math that we bring home about $1,000 per week, or around $25 per hour. In this example, a new pair of $200 shoes costs us the equivalent of an eight-hour working day. Most of us, though, don't make the calculations to link our time to the time it costs to pay for the stuff so we don't think about whether it was worth eight hours of work to buy a pair of shoes or how many years of work we commit to when we buy a house.

To change this bias, we can start calculating how much time we have to spend working for the material goods in our life. That will give us the time "cost" of our purchases. It also helps us consider what we're working *for* and whether it's aligned with our priorities. We can decide if we want our eight hours of labor to go toward the purchase of a pair of shoes or the purchase of a night out with our significant other or friends or toward something else on our priorities list.

Reclaiming Your Time

The insights from the calendar diagnostic should give you ideas about how to restructure your time to better align with your priorities. Time-use studies suggest that we're not as busy as we say we are. We like to complain that we have no time, but evidence indicates that we fritter away the time we do have. The Bureau of Labor Statistics ongoing Time Use Survey shows that we have an average of five to six hours of leisure time per day.[4] We spend over half of that time watching TV and have done so persistently for the past half decade.

When we aren't glued to the TV, it seems we're busy because we choose to be. Tim Kreider captured this phenomenon best in his *New York Times* essay "The 'Busy' Trap":

> It's almost always people whose lamented busyness is purely self-imposed: work and obligations they've taken on voluntarily, classes and activities they've "encouraged" their kids to participate in. They're busy because of their own ambition or drive or anxiety, because they're addicted to busyness and dread what they might have to face in its absence. . . . The present hysteria is not a necessary or inevitable condition of life; it's something we've chosen, if only by our acquiescence to it.[5]

If we feel persistently overwhelmed, harried, and stressed about how we spend our time, it's likely that we're not spending it in a way that's aligned with our values and priorities. To transition to investing in our priorities, we need to develop a plan to clear our schedules of existing obligations that we no longer want to continue. The following strategies, which I call the 4 Ds, can help clear space on our calendar.

Drop it: As Arianna Huffington says, you can complete a project by dropping it.[6] Some commitments you can just withdraw from or stop doing. "No" is still a complete sentence.

Diminish it: Reduce the frequency or size of the commitment. Keep volunteering at your favorite nonprofit, but roll off the board. Instead of taking a 30-minute meeting plus travel time, schedule a 15-minute phone call.

Defer it: This approach kicks the can to the future, but as you undertake restructuring your time, you may find it helpful not to deal with all of your existing obligations at once. Push out a few commitments and give yourself some breathing room to further evaluate how you want to handle them.

Delegate it: The combination of the Gig Economy and technology has made it much easier and convenient to delegate as a way to save and make the best use of our time. We can't do everything, so as much as possible we want to invest in activities that align with our priorities and that require our specific attention, skills, and talent. Purchasing help is buying time, and it works best if the time we're buying is meaningfully cheaper than what we're paid for the time we sell. But cost isn't the only consideration. Tasks that are particularly time consuming, inconvenient, or physically demanding or involve doing things that we really dislike are all candidates for outsourcing.

Delegating errands and chores and outsourcing the tedium of daily life used to be accessible only to the wealthy. The companies that make up the Staff Economy, such as Uber, TaskRabbit, Postmates, Handy, and Instacart, have lowered the price of help dramatically and disrupted the economics of outsourcing tasks in urban areas. Those of us in less-dense areas might have to do more of our physical chores (or work harder or pay more to outsource them) but can still delegate administrative work, such as scheduling, email, and organizational tasks to a remote assistant here or abroad or to a freelancer on Upwork.

Technology can also be a source of low-to-no-cost delegation and help limit the time we spend on tedious chores. For example, if a virtual assistant is beyond your budget, scheduling tools like Doodle, ScheduleOnce, or YouCanBook.me reduce the time it takes to schedule meetings and respond to requests while also eliminating multiple back and forths, long email threads, and double bookings.

Bartering is a final form of delegating. Take your love of gardening and being outdoors and offer to do your neighbor's spring garden while, in exchange, she releases her inner germophobe and does your spring housecleaning. The accountant in my family is able to barter his tax preparation services in exchange for plumbing, handyman help, and snowplowing his driveway during the winter. Everybody wins and nobody has to pay. Bartering is a perfect way to do the things you love in exchange for the things you hate.

Once you have time and space cleared on your calendar by implementing the 4 Ds—Drop it, Diminish It, Defer It or Delegate It—you can begin to think about restructuring and reallocating your time going forward.

Rebuilding Your Calendar:
Manager vs. Maker Schedule

Compressing too many activities into too little time makes it difficult to achieve our most meaningful goals. We can't deepen our connections with others and devote significant attention to our important relationships if we're also checking email or watching the clock because we're scheduled for something else in 10 minutes. To be our most effective and efficient selves and to create the time to invest in our priorities, we need reasonably sized blocks of time.

One way to create that time is to apply the framework of Maker vs. Manager schedules to our calendars. Paul Graham of Y Combinator introduced the concept in his 2009 blog post "Maker's Schedule, Manager's Schedule."[7] I'll summarize the concepts he introduces, but it's worth reading it in its entirety.

The Manager's Schedule

The Manager's Schedule is the one most familiar to us, as it's common for traditional employees and management (as the name implies) in corporations. The day is structured around half-hour to one-hour blocks of time, in which meetings and phone calls take place throughout the day. Following is an example of what a Manager's Schedule calendar can look like.[8] In a Manager's Schedule, workdays are double booked and chopped into intervals of an hour or half-hour.

Some jobs are largely Manager's Schedule jobs. If you're a salesperson, you don't need huge blocks of time to do creative work. What you need is short chunks of time for interactions like phone calls, emailing, and visiting potential customers.

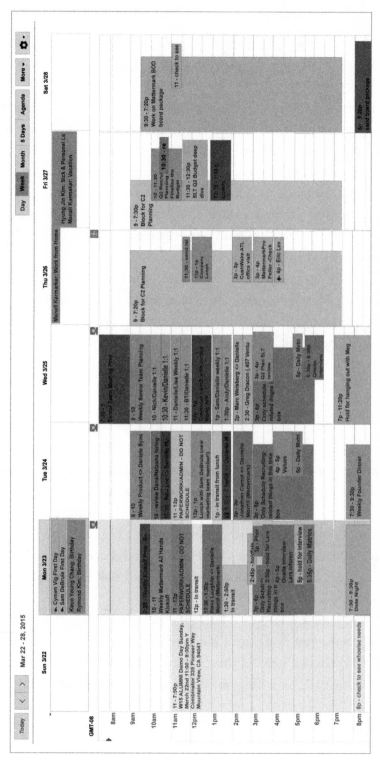

Source: medium.com/@DanielleMorrill/warming-up-to-the-manager-s-schedule-e3ec18c7408#.mkhds7o74 (Used with permission)

Relationship-intensive and highly interactive jobs are often better suited to a Manager's Schedule.

The Maker's Schedule

The Maker's Schedule is for anyone who needs blocks of focused time to think and strategize or complete tasks and projects, which is many of us. It's designed to leave some or all of the day free of any interruptions or commitments to allow the space and time to settle into a complex project and work on it. Any calls or meetings are grouped together and scheduled into designated time blocks so that the rest of the working day is left clear.

If you hold a full-time corporate job that requires the Manager's Schedule but need creative or focused time, consider implementing a Maker's Schedule one or two days a week, blocking off a minimum of a half day and retreating to a conference room or working from home to tackle a larger or longer-term project. We can also create our own Maker's Schedule outside of our full-time jobs by scheduling uninterrupted blocks of time early in the morning, later at night, or on weekends.

Two colleagues of mine have, at different times, created their own Maker's Schedule to study for the six-hour Chartered Financial Analyst (CFA) Level 1 Exam, the first in a series of three rigorous tests needed to become a CFA charterholder. On average, professionals preparing for the exam spend about 300 hours studying for it. My colleagues each had young families and full-time jobs tied to a Manager's Schedule, so they weren't able to carve a block of time out of their workday schedule or evening and weekend time. Instead, to make the time to study, they came into the office from 5:30 a.m. to 8 a.m. each morning. They kept up this routine over several months. There's little that is easy or attractive about their schedule, and it certainly required some negotiating on the home front to execute, but it gave each of them the blocks of time they needed to study and prepare. And, yes, they both passed!

Whether the Manager's or Maker's Schedule, or a hybrid, is right for you, rebuilding your calendar from scratch can be a useful way to reallocate and reprioritize your time. Start with a blank month and start filling in dedicated "blocks" of time that represent investments of time into your top priorities. Start filling in the most important, high-priority tasks and activities and continue from there.

Starting with a clean month and blocking time for specific activities forces us to be ruthlessly definitive about what matters. This exercise is best done first on our own and then with someone else—a coworker or boss for our work calendar and our spouse or a close friend for our family/personal calendar. A second set of eyes can bring the perspective and distance to help us identify commitments of time that we don't seem enthusiastic about or that we've accepted due to pressure, guilt, or a false sense of obligation.

This is an example of a rebuilt calendar incorporating a Maker's Schedule. The designated blocks of time represent priorities during the day.

Building a calendar from the ground up is a valuable exercise for clarifying our priorities in our minds as well as on our schedules. The examples so far have included only a restructuring of work time, but the exercise is best done by allocating and structuring all of our time to incorporate our personal priorities and commitments.

The Corporate Time Suck

Moving from a Manager's to a Maker's Schedule isn't easy. Even if a Maker's Schedule would be a better fit for the work

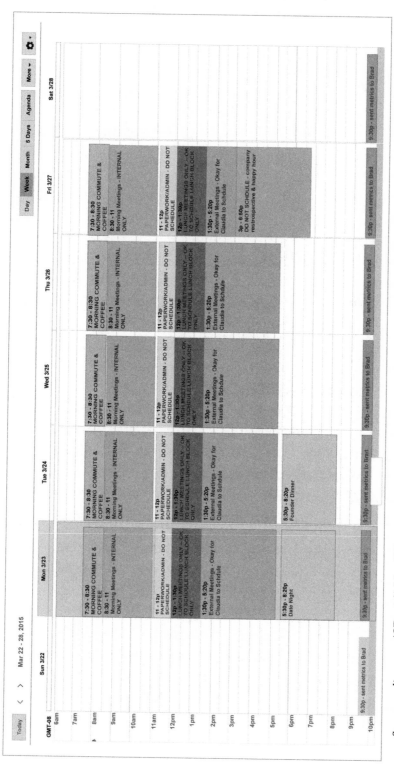

Source: medium.com/@DanielleMorrill/warming-up-to-the-manager-s-schedule-e3ec18c7408e#.mkhds7o74 (Used with permission)

that you do, it can be difficult to implement if you work full-time for a company.

Most companies are incredibly poor stewards of their time. They obsessively track and limit employee hours out of the office—vacation time, paid time off, and even remote work time—yet once the employee is physically in the office there are virtually no cost controls, limits, or oversights to manage employee time. Corporate time sucks like email, conference calls, and meetings aren't monitored or tracked (despite the availability of technology to do so), so they freely multiply and expand to fill the vacuum of the workday. Open-space offices and open-door policies guarantee interruptions and distractions that can make it difficult and inefficient to get work done. Given the uncontrolled, unmanaged, anything-goes approach to time management at most firms, it may be nearly impossible to swim against the tide of corporate norms to implement your own Maker-like time-management system.

It can also be difficult to change time-management practices because many employees have *learned helplessness* about their time at the office. Learned helplessness is a psychological phenomenon that arises when people are forced to endure negative events or negative consequences over which they have no control. In the classic demonstration of learned helplessness:

> [S]ubjects are randomly divided into three groups. Those in the first are exposed to an annoying loud noise that they can stop by pushing a button in front of them. Those in the second hear the same noise but can't turn it off, though they try hard. Those in the third, the control group, hear nothing at all. Later, typically the following day, the subjects are faced with a brand-new situation that again involves noise. To turn the noise off, all they have to do is move their hands about 12 inches. The people in the first and third groups

figure this out and readily learn to avoid the noise. But those in the second group typically do nothing. In phase one they failed, realized they had no control, and became passive. In phase two, expecting more failure, they don't even try to escape. They have learned helplessness.[9]

Employees who attempt to strategically manage their time at the office can have the same experience. If employees don't attend meetings or refuse to put in face time, corporations respond with the equivalent of the loud noise we can't shut off—lack of flexibility, lack of support, and reprimands. Eventually, expecting more failure, employees don't even try to optimize their time.

The result is that high costs and inefficiencies accrue. Employees become dissatisfied with rigid schedules that force them to work in ways that are inefficient or less productive and acquire poor time-management habits. Fortunately, the Gig Economy offers us options for escaping this lose-lose dysfunction of the corporate time suck.

Independent workers retain autonomy, control, and flexibility over their workday and are reasonably free to schedule and allocate their time to maximize their productivity and results. The Gig Economy values skills above all, so in-demand talent, strong performers, and employees with a good exit strategy are also well positioned to retain control of their workday time. They have the least to lose by disregarding corporate norms and managing their own time in their own way.

Expanding Time

All of this work diagnosing, restructuring, and rebuilding our calendars can help us better invest and allocate our time to our most important priorities. What it can't do is change how much time we actually have, but there are ways we can change how much time we perceive we have. Feeling like we have more time can help us feel less busy, more relaxed, and more present. There are a number of ways we can create a feeling of having more time:

Expand Time by Engaging in New Experiences

We're all painfully aware of how time seems to speed up as we age. Those endless summer days we enjoyed as a kid now pass in the blink of an eye as an adult. David Eagleman, a neuroscientist at Baylor College of Medicine, explains this age-related difference in time perception.[10] His research demonstrates that new experiences take more time for our brains to process than familiar ones, making our perception of that time seem longer. As we age, more and more of our experiences are familiar and processed quickly, which makes time seem faster. We perceive that time is flying by. To slow down time, engage in new experiences. Keep learning, meet new people, travel to places you've never been to, and challenge yourself to try new activities. Time will seem to pass more slowly (and be more interesting).

Expand Time by Becoming Powerful

People in relative power positions—boss vs. employee or interviewer vs. interviewee—feel like they have more time. Research from the University of California, Berkeley found that high-power individuals perceived that they had more time, partly due to the perception that they have more control over their time. The implications for the Gig Economy are positive. As we take more control of our time, and assume the less-powerful role of employee less frequently, we should begin to feel like we have more time available.[11]

Expand Time by Giving Time Away

If we're already feeling short on time, it seems counterintuitive to recommend giving it away by helping others or by volunteering. But a recent psychological study from the University of Pennsylvania's Wharton School found that giving our time to help others leaves us less stressed and hurried and feeling like we have more time. The reason is that people who give their time feel more "capable, confident, and useful" and feel like they've accomplished something. This overall feeling of self-efficacy makes time feel expansive, and it arises even when we spend very short amounts of time (just 10 minutes!) helping others.[12]

Expand Time by Combining Physical and Mental Tasks

Human brains are not optimized for multitasking. The exception is multitasking that uses different sensory channels, such as going for a walk while listening to a podcast or talking to a friend while doing the dishes. By combining a physical activities such as walking or chores with mental ones such as listening or talking, we can accomplish both efficiently and effectively.

BEING MINDFUL ABOUT TIME IS THE NEW BUSY

The Gig Economy gives us greater opportunity to take greater ownership of our time and align our time with our priorities.

As you contemplate restructuring your time, consider:

▸ How can I spend time in ways that are more aligned with my priorities?

➤ Could I better align my time and priorities by considering the Maker/Manager framework and by rebuilding my calendar?

➤ How can I expand my time so I feel less busy?

Part Three

FINANCING THE LIFE
You Want

· Chapter Eight ·

BE FINANCIALLY FLEXIBLE

The American Paradox:

More than ever, we at the end of the last century were finding ourselves with big houses and broken homes, high incomes and low morale . . . We were excelling at making a living but too often failing at making a life. We celebrated our prosperity but yearned for purpose. We cherished our freedoms but longed for connection. In an age of plenty, we were feeling spiritual hunger.

—DAVID MYERS

The Gig Economy requires us to reconsider how we think about money. A high fixed-cost lifestyle financed with debt might be sustainable (although not ideal) in an economy of steady paychecks and long-term secure jobs, but we don't live in that world anymore. No job is secure, and we can expect our income to vary over our working lives. To succeed in the Gig Economy, we need to create a financially flexible life of lower fixed costs, higher savings, and much less debt.

When I teach the financial section of my MBA Gig Economy course, there are always some students who come to realize that they're paying for a life they don't want. The consequences of that realization are occasionally dramatic. I've had graduates make significant moves from the suburbs to the city or to another part of the country. Several have quit jobs, turned down job offers, or dropped out of recruiting for postgraduate employment. They've taken pay cuts to do work they enjoy, they've gone traveling, or they've started their own businesses. A few have even asked me to meet with them and their spouses to facilitate a discussion about completely restructuring their families' lives.

This section is not an incremental, save-your-latte-money approach to financial planning. It is both deeper and broader than that. Deeper in the sense that the goal is to structure a financial plan aligned with your priorities and values, not just cut spending. Broader in that we'll look at options to increase income and savings, in addition to reducing expenses. The save-your-latte-money school of thought takes a mostly one-sided view of managing money by focusing almost entirely on cutting expenses and hardly at all on generating more income. It's the all-diet-no-exercise approach to financial health that we'll avoid.

Too much financial advice avoids confronting the reality that although our financial lives are affected by small daily decisions, the biggest choices we make are the ones that create or destroy our financial health. Cutting back on your morning lattes or bringing your lunch to work every day instead of eating out will save money, but the amount pales in comparison to what you spend on a mortgage and car payments. Housing and transportation are the big-ticket financial choices that make up about half of the average family's expenditures.[1]

If you want to transform your financial life, start by evaluating your biggest financial choices, not your smallest ones.

Robert is a good example of someone who evaluated and restructured his financial life. Robert was a vice president at a large Midwestern company until he was unexpectedly laid off as part of a company-wide reduction in force. He received a severance package that gave him "the financial runway to breathe," but the runway wasn't long, and he was anxious about getting his next job. He had three young kids, a large mortgage, and was the sole breadwinner. He began applying vigorously for jobs and following any lead that seemed like it would result in a well-paying position and a renewed feeling of financial security for himself, his wife, and his kids.

The turning point in his search came when a call he and I had unexpectedly turned into a conversation about the core questions that Robert realized he needed to address: What type of work did he want to do? Where did he want to live? What were his priorities? What did he want his family life to look like for the next decade?

Robert and his wife began, for the first time in a long time, having conversations about the fundamental structure of their lives: What values were most important to them? What kind of family experience did they want to create for their children? How important were traditional measures of material and financial success to them? What *really* mattered to them? Their answers, it turned out, weren't consistent with the life they were living.

That realization led them to begin restructuring their lives from the top down. They decided to move back home to Kansas City to be near their extended family, which was an important priority for them but one they hadn't been fulfilling. They sold their large home in an upscale St. Louis suburb and downsized to a much more modest home in Kansas City. Many people see downsizing as a negative outcome, but Robert couldn't disagree more. For him, downsizing created a sense of financial security and freedom in his family's life. It helped him gain a feeling of control over his financial life that has lowered his anxiety, reduced his financial dependence on his job, and allowed his family to begin traveling together on a regular basis, which Robert and his wife had decided was an important experience (and set of memories) they wanted to give their children.

Two years after leaving the company, Robert and his family are much happier and more secure in their new life in Kansas City. He says, "I'm much more financially and emotionally prepared for my next transition, and my life is much more aligned with my priorities." Like Robert, your version of the American Dream might be cheaper and involve a lot less debt than the traditional version. You might also be willing to downsize to gain flexibility and focus on your priorities. Having "enough" money to live the American Dream depends on what your version of that dream is.

In the end, a good financial plan isn't about reducing your spending per se; it's about making sure that you spend what you have in a way that is meaningful to you.

Before discussing ways to change your financial life, it makes sense to assess where you are today. Bearing in mind the quote from chapter 7 that "between the calendar and checkbook, one's priorities are laid bare," this exercise asks you to perform a "checkbook diagnostic" to help you evaluate the alignment between your priorities and spending.

EXERCISE

A Checkbook Diagnostic

STEP 1: REVISIT MY PRIORITIES

The first step is to consider your responses to three key questions raised in the exercise in chapter 1:

◆ What does success look like to me?

- What are the values and priorities I want to live?
- What is my definition of a good job, a good career, and, even, a good life?

STEP 2: AUDIT MY SPENDING

Gather the data on your spending from wherever you track it (your Quicken dashboard, Mint.com, your credit card statements, your bank statements, or your checkbook; if you don't track it, start to do so using one of these tools). Go back through the past year and review how you spent your money. Answer the following questions:

- What were my five biggest financial commitments each month and for the year?
- What did I spend my money on? Break spending into categories to help see where it's going and evaluate your largest categories.
- What life am I buying?
- Is this the life I want?

STEP 3: EVALUATE IF MY SPENDING IS ALIGNED WITH MY PRIORITIES

Step back and reflect on these questions:

- How much alignment is there between my priorities and spending?
- Do my five biggest financial commitments move me closer to or further away from a life aligned with my priorities?

Be concrete in your answers: If a top priority for you is family, how much money did you spend on experiences together (outings, vacations, dinners together, family memberships, etc.)

compared to individual activities? If there is misalignment, consider:

◆ What changes can I make, and am I willing to make, to better align my money and my priorities?

If you're like Robert and you already feel like your life is in sync with your priorities, then Chuzzah! Congratulations, this chapter will be an easy review for you.

Otherwise, once you've revisited your priorities and conducted the checkbook diagnostic, you can use the rest of this chapter to explore concrete ways to restructure your finances and increase financial flexibility in your own life.

Increase Financial Flexibility by Making More Money

The Gig Economy presents us with numerous opportunities to generate additional income on our own schedule. We can monetize side gigs (which we discussed in detail in chapter 8), rent our existing assets (e.g., list a bedroom on Airbnb), or pursue on-demand gig opportunities like bidding for gigs on Upwork or Experfy or finding work on HourlyNerd. It has never been easier, or more convenient, to work incremental hours on our own schedule and generate incremental income.

One strategy, whether we're employed at a job or working independently, is to persistently watch for opportunities to increase our income. If we're in a traditional full-time job, we should periodically assess the possibility of negotiating a raise or a performance-based bonus or positioning for a promotion. If our current job doesn't offer many opportunities for growth or advancement, consider changing jobs as a way to take on more responsibility or increase compensation.

Another strategy, if we're working as a contractor or consultant is to regularly check our pricing strategy against prevailing market rates. It's common in the early days of working independently or starting a service business to charge below-market rates to attract customers and build a client base. By charging lower prices it's easier to win clients and gain the experience we need to build up our references, improve our reputation, and better position us for future work. When we realize we have too much demand for our services and can turn down opportunities, it could mean it's time to raise rates.

A final strategy is to consider shifting our target customer so we can target larger companies or bid on bigger projects.

Theresa was able to increase her coaching business revenues by executing the last two of these strategies. She began her coaching career at midlife after she left her corporate job, became certified as a coach, and started her own business. As a new coach, she built her business by charging below-market rates and working primarily with individuals. This strategy worked, and she was soon busy with an almost-full client roster. Deciding she wanted to increase her revenues and work more with business leaders, Theresa raised her rates and began targeting small and midsize companies, where she could win engagements working with several members of an executive team. It's a strategy that worked. She has developed a specialty working with women business leaders and entrepreneurs and charges at or above market rates for her services. She makes more money working with fewer, larger clients.

So far we've talked only about increasing our income from working (also called *earned income*) versus investing (or *unearned income*). Most Americans generate their compensation from earned income. Analysis from the Urban-Brookings Tax Policy

Center shows that 64 percent of Americans earn their income from a paycheck.[2] It's possible to achieve financial security and comfort through earned income, but it's difficult to become wealthy because our earned income is limited by the finite hours of our labor we can sell.

Passive income, or unearned income, comes from our investments—in real estate, the stock market, and businesses. It's this investment income that most often creates wealth. The Urban-Brookings study found that the top 1 percent of Americans earn the majority (53 percent) of their income from passive sources rather than from a paycheck. It's more volatile, and higher risk, than earned income but offers potentially higher reward. Passive income is produced by renting our homes or owning a piece of a business through direct ownership or through stock options or employee stock that many companies grant their employees. We can generate passive income from investing our retirement and savings account in the stock market. Looking for work at a company that offers equity compensation is another way to increase passive income, as is renting out any real estate you own or rent. As you consider options for making more money, consider ways you can earn more from your labor as well as generating passive income.

Increase Financial Flexibility by Stashing the Cash

Savings give us flexibility, create options in our life, and cushion the blow of unexpected financial setbacks like a job loss or unanticipated expense. With savings set aside, we can consider quitting that tedious job and then taking time to find the right next step. We can plan that memorable family vacation, stay home with our kids, go to our best friend's destination wedding, and have the financial ability to make other decisions that matter to us. We can also weather unexpected setbacks more easily. A surprise health expense or car repair won't become a crisis if we have savings in the bank. Savings give us flexibility and choice. The way to build those savings quickly and consistently is to live below our means, all the time, forever. Stop buying lattes if you wish and save three dollars a day, but there are other higher-impact ways to live below your means.

Stash the Cash by Living on One Salary

If you're part of a dual-income couple or family, one of the most impactful financial decisions you can make is to live entirely on one paycheck while saving the other. Living on one paycheck frees up the other paycheck to accelerate your rate of savings, pay down debt, or build up your financial cushion. Living on just one income also prevents you from too rapidly increasing your lifestyle beyond what you can sustainably earn.

Let's say you're part of a couple and each of you makes $75,000 per year, for a household income of $150,000. Assuming a total tax rate of 30 percent, you take home $52,500 each. If you live on just one salary, you could save (or pay down debt or invest) more than $50,000 per year. It's a powerful strategy.

Stash the Cash by Banking the Windfalls

If your career is going well, you might find yourself in the fortunate position of receiving more income than expected due to bonuses, raises, winning an extra project, or being awarded an extra few months of work or an unexpected project from a key client. Sometimes life steps in with a cash surprise, from an unexpected tax refund, a monetary gift, an inheritance, or a severance payout. When these prosperous events occur, get into the habit of automatically banking the unplanned extra cash that you receive. Saving most or all of those windfalls can beef up your cash reserves or make a big dent in your debt putting you ahead of schedule in accomplishing your financial goals.

Stash the Cash by Making the Most of Corporate Perks

The times we spend working a traditional full-time job are great opportunities to save. Even if we earn the same income as when we were working independently, our expenses will be lower.

When we work full time, our tax rate is lower than when we work independently since we're no longer paying employer taxes. This lower tax rate combined with a steady paycheck creates a good opportunity to set up an automatic plan to save a fixed percent each pay period.

Our insurance and benefits costs tend to be lower when we're an employee. We also tend to have better insurance coverage, so we can take advantage of that to schedule all of our basic healthcare and checkups during this time to minimize our out-of-pocket costs.

Working a full-time corporate job can give us access to a range of benefits. We can take advantage of the 401(k) retirement plan match that most companies offer, as well as the benefits of paid time off and reimbursement for education, training, and other professional development and connection opportunities, such as attending conferences. If you're working a full-time job, maximize your use of the benefits offered.

Increase Financial Flexibility by Keeping Your Personal Burn Rate Low

In the startup world, investors and entrepreneurs talk about a company's monthly *burn rate*, which is the net amount of money the company spends each month, or the negative cash flow. For instance, a young tech company that hasn't started generating revenues, with expenses of $25,000 per month, has a burn rate of $25,000 per month. If the company generates revenues of $20,000 per month, its burn rate would be $5,000 per month. The way to maximize financial flexibility is to keep your burn rate low.

EXERCISE

Determine Your Personal Burn Rate

STEP 1: TALLY YOUR SAVINGS

Add up any liquid savings, including cash in the bank, short-term CDs, and investments in stocks/mutual funds (not including retirement accounts).

STEP 2: DETERMINE YOUR PERSONAL BURN RATE

Using the financial information you have already gathered for the Checkbook Diagnostic, sum the total of all your expenses by month and for the year. The sum of your expenses is your burn rate (we're assuming for the purposes of this step that you have no income because you are in between gigs and not working).

Divide your savings from Step 1 by your monthly personal burn rate from Step 2, and you have a preliminary idea of how many months you could live your current lifestyle if you earned no income. It's a proxy for how much financial flexibility you have in your life. The more months you can cover your expenses, the more flexibility you have.

STEP 3: UNDERSTAND YOUR PERSONAL BURN RATE

Answer the following questions to better identify what drives your personal burn rate.

- What are my top expenses?
- Can I reduce or eliminate any of those commitments or habits?
- What is the minimum burn rate I could achieve immediately if I had to?
- What is the minimum burn rate I could achieve with six months of planning?

STEP 4: CALCULATE YOUR FINANCIAL FLEXIBILITY

To complete the exercise, compare your current monthly income with your current personal burn rate. Answer the following questions:

- How much income do I need to earn to cover my personal burn rate and still have money available to save?
- Am I living above or below my means?
- By how much?

This exercise will help you get a preliminary sense of the level of financial flexibility and financial security in your life.

If your personal burn rate is high, you need to generate a high level of income to live at or above it. A high burn rate can limit your financial flexibility. If your burn rate is low, you have more flexibility to generate variable income and still live at or above your means. You are more financially flexible and more financially secure.

Increase Financial Flexibility by Creating a Financial Plan

In the uncertain environment of the Gig Economy, a financial plan is essential. Research shows that across income levels, households that engage in financial planning are more likely to save for emergencies, save for retirement, have adequate insurance, and manage debt.[3] Yet very few Americans have one. Less than half of U.S. households (38 percent) complete even a minimal amount of planning to achieve specific goals like saving for retirement or college. Only a small minority, just 19 percent of households, have a comprehensive financial plan that includes a budget, taxes, insurance, and savings.[4] Interestingly, the majority of this group of comprehensive planners reports an annual household income below $100,000.

Independent workers in the Gig Economy have more financial management responsibilities than the average household. We need a plan to cover volatile income streams and periods of unemployment. If we do contract work or consulting, we're responsible for paying our own taxes, buying health insurance, sending invoices, collecting payments, and managing, tracking, and deducting expenses.

It doesn't have to take much time or money to create and implement a financial plan, nor do you have to do it yourself. Consulting with a personal financial team can be a good way to create, implement, and monitor a plan. Your financial team should include the following members.

A fee-only financial planner: Meeting with a fee-only financial planner once per year can help add structure and accountability to your financial plan. Fee-only planners charge by the hour (generally ranging from $150 to $500 per hour) or a flat fee per plan. If you already use online tools to manage your finances, they can help reduce the cost of a planner. The cost of a comprehensive financial plan from scratch varies depending on the complexity of your situation but generally speaking falls in the $1,000 to $4,000 range. The initial plan will cost the most due to the setup time, and then the subsequent annual meetings should be less. Look for a planner that specializes in or has worked with self-employed clients and understands how to create a financial plan around variable income.

An accountant: Schedule an initial meeting with an accountant when you first start, or plan to start, working independently. An accountant can advise you on how best to structure yourself. Many independent workers operate simply as a sole proprietor, which doesn't require any particular legal structure. Others find it beneficial to do business as a Limited Liability Corporation (LLC) or as an S Corp. Deciding whether to structure as a sole proprietor, LLC, or S Corp depends on the type of work you do, what state you live in, and what percentage of your compensation is supplied by Gig Economy work. An accountant can help you evaluate these options and assess the tax impact of each based on your situation.

As an independent worker, you're responsible for withholding and filing your own federal and state taxes quarterly.

Meeting with an accountant annually can help you estimate the amount of tax you should pay and set up a schedule (and reminders!) to ensure you file and pay on time. Independent workers can also deduct a variety of expenses against their income. Your accountant can help you understand which expenses you should be separately tracking and deducting throughout the year.

A bookkeeper: Many independent workers in-source this function by using QuickBooks or a similar tool to track their income and expenses. Others prefer to outsource to a bookkeeper. No matter which approach you choose, the idea is to maintain a system for maintaining your financial records, tracking deductions and expenses, and managing invoicing and collections. Depending on the complexity of your business, your level of organization, and how much you can automate, an experienced bookkeeper can cost anywhere from $30 to $150 an hour.

There are also online options to help with financial planning, taxes, and expenses. Tools like Mint.com and Learn-Vest can help you begin your financial planning process, and apps like Expensify, Xero, and Qapital can be used to track and manage expenses or increase savings. Existing companies like Intuit (makers of TurboTax), AND CO, and FreshBooks are developing tools targeted to independent workers to manage taxes, expenses, budgeting, and invoicing. As the Gig Economy grows, we can expect to see more apps and startups create tools to help manage the back office and financial planning needs of independent workers.

FINANCIAL FLEXIBILITY IS
THE NEW LIVING PAYCHECK TO PAYCHECK

Succeeding in the Gig Economy requires us to be financially flexible and implement a different, more deliberate approach to managing money. Without a steady paycheck, we have to rethink and restructure our financial lives to align our spending with our priorities, consistently live below our means, rigorously manage our biggest expenses, and save at unprecedented levels.

To increase your own financial flexibility, consider:

- ▶ What are my biggest financial decisions and commitments?
- ▶ How much alignment is there between my spending and my priorities?
- ▶ Are there ways I can make more money, or stash more cash?
- ▶ What are the best ways for me to keep my personal burn rate low?

• Chapter Nine •

THINK ACCESS,
NOT OWNERSHIP

Normal is getting dressed in clothes that you buy for
work and driving through traffic in a car that you are still
paying for—in order to get to the job you need to pay for
the clothes and the car, and the house you leave vacant
all day so you can afford to live in it.

—ELLEN GOODMAN

The newfound possibilities in the Gig Economy to access instead of own represent nothing short of a personal financial revolution. It transforms the underlying economics of our lives. The
option to rent, not buy, to access, not own, increases our control
over how and what we consume, is more flexible, and can save
us money. It's also more convenient and offers more variety. We
no longer need to spend large amounts of money or take on
significant debt to purchase and own. We can pay less for access
on demand and use the difference to save, invest, or buy time.
My former student Ben summed it up best:

Many of the things in my life that I previously would have
purchased are now borrowed for the short period of time
that I have a use for them. I stream music and movies and
rent electronic copies of books. I use Hubway to commute to
work and rent the apartment in which I live. While I may

have been resistant to this idea of limited ownership a few years ago, it has become a part of my daily life and I now embrace it. Renting an item gives much greater flexibility and access while providing a sense of freedom from the clutter and headaches of ownership.

Ownership isn't dead and it isn't likely to completely die, but it can be deferred or discretionary in a way that's unprecedented historically. The Gig Economy gives us options to rent or access cars (Zipcar, Uber), bikes (Hubway, Citi Bike), fully furnished apartments and homes (Airbnb, Onefinestay), clothes (Rent the Runway, Le Tote), jewelry (Haute Vault), and just about anything else. With the ability to access so much so easily, we need to come up with pretty compelling reasons to buy.

There's even a lifestyle emerging built on the foundation of the access economy. Prerna Gupta, a serial entrepreneur, wrote about her experience living what she calls "the Airbnb lifestyle."[1] She and her husband lived in several countries over the course of the year, staying in temporary Airbnb housing in every location and carrying all of their possessions in a few suitcases. Her experience made her question the need to return to a traditional home-based life and led to a "palpable change" in her relationship with her possessions. She believes that the Airbnb lifestyle will become more common in part due to the changes in how we work. "Work is becoming much more fluid, and workers have increasing control over when and where they work. This makes them less tied down." Owning, after all, reduces flexibility.

The ability to access instead of own is not yet equally available. Urban areas offer the greatest opportunity to reduce our levels of ownership, particularly since both transportation and housing, which are the largest expenses in most households, can be more easily accessed (rented) in cities. We can significantly increase our financial flexibility just by turning these two large fixed costs into equal-sized or smaller variable expenses.

This geographic dispersion in the ability to access goods and services is inverting the relative cost of life in the suburbs versus the city. The suburbs, with their high fixed costs, ownership-dominated lifestyle, and limited offerings of on-demand goods and services, start to seem disproportionately expensive. As cities transform into access economies where goods and services are flexible, convenient, and available on demand, they become more attractive to Gig Economy workers on variable, unstable incomes.

Ownership and the Thief of Debt

Perspectives on debt have changed in the Gig Economy. Financial experts used to talk about the differences between "good debt," such as mortgages and student loans, and "bad debt," including car loans and credit card balances. This distinction has become less relevant because in the Gig Economy it's become so much riskier to carry any debt. It's hard to make the case for committing to high fixed-debt payments in an economy of insecure jobs and variable income.

Whether it's good or bad, debt always increases your risk, robs you of flexibility, and appropriates your options. It can limit your ability to change jobs, move, start your own business, or take time off. It claims your financial future. In the worst case, debt forces you to build a lifestyle around supporting your payments instead of around your priorities and goals.

America is a highly indebted nation. We regularly take on "bad debt" to buy goods that rapidly depreciate in value. We pay high fees on credit cards and loans to buy cars, consumer goods, jewelry, and clothing, little of which we need, much of which we want, all of which starts losing value as soon as we walk out of the store. But our largest debt doesn't come from Saturdays at the mall or the car dealership. The biggest sources of debt in the United States arise from taking on the "good debt" of mortgages and student loans.[2] Let's look at these further.

The Truth about Home Ownership

The benefits of access over ownership seem clear for consumer goods that we don't use every day. But how does it work for the very large and very expensive purchase of a home? Does ownership make more sense then? Aren't mortgages "good debt"?

For many Americans, the decision to buy a home isn't primarily financial. Instead, it's based on emotional and personal factors. If where or how we live is high on our list of personal priorities, then we might be willing to incur some financial underperformance to achieve our particular vision of home life. We might want to buy or own, for sentimental reasons, the house that's been in our family for decades, even if needs a lot of costly work. Not every house-buying decision is a purely financial one, but even then, it still makes sense to clearly understand the financial consequences of those choices.

Evaluated solely as a financial decision, homeownership is a risky investment. Houses are highly leveraged, mostly illiquid, very expensive, and immovable assets. Any objective financial assessment would conclude that it makes sense to hold an asset with those characteristics only as a small percent of a larger, mostly liquid, and lower-risk portfolio. But that's not what happens in the United States.

Home Ownership Is Killing the Middle Class

Edward Wolff, an economist at New York University, studies wealth distribution and the impact of home ownership of the wealthiest 1 percent of Americans compared to the next 19 percent, which he calls the *upper middle class*, and the middle 60 percent, which he calls the *broad middle class*. His results are alarming:[3]

- Nearly two thirds of the wealth of middle class Americans is in their homes: a very highly concentrated and highly risky state of financial affairs. The broad middle class has 63 percent of their net worth (assets minus debt) in their principal residence. In contrast, the upper middle class has a much more diverse portfolio, with a little under one third (28 percent) of their net worth in their homes. The top 1 percent tie up only 9 percent of their net worth in their primary residence.

- According to Wolff, both the increasing gap in wealth inequality and the financially fragile state of the middle class stems from their overinvestment in their homes. The overconcentration in housing and the high levels of debt the middle class carry in their homes hurt them badly in the Great Recession and housing crisis of 2008. Wolff looked particularly at the years 2007 to 2013 to assess the impact of these two events and found that they hurt the broad middle class the most: "The sharp fall in median net worth and the rise in overall wealth inequality over these years are traceable primarily to the high leverage of middle-class families and the high share of homes in their portfolio."

- A recent report from the Pew Research Center also concluded that the differences in the percentage of housing that the upper and middle classes hold in their portfolios are increasing the wealth gap. It concluded that "the disparate trends in the wealth of middle-income and upper-income families are due to the fact that housing assumes a greater role in the portfolios of middle-income families."[4] The report notes that upper-income families had three times as much wealth as middle-income families in 1983 but ended 2013 with more than seven times as much.

Middle-class Americans are overinvested in housing, and that investment is not paying off. Housing has delivered persistently low rates of return relative to other asset classes like stocks and mutual funds.[5] The middle class has overinvested in an asset that underperforms. The long-term rate of return (from 1983–2013) for financial assets like stocks has been about 9 percent, compared to the 3.5 percent return on residential real estate over that same time period. During the Great Recession and housing crisis (2007–2010), residential real estate returns fell by about 7 percent, twice as much as financial assets returns, which declined by only 3.7 percent. And real estate has been slow to recover. After the recession, from 2010–2013, residential real estate returned nearly 5 percent, but financial assets have delivered more than double the returns—over 12 percent.

In every economic scenario—long term, crash, and recovery—it's been better to hold financial assets than residential real estate. Yet the broad middle class holds only 3 percent of its assets in stocks and mutual funds, compared to holding over 60 percent of its net worth in housing. The returns data here is clear: If you're looking for returns, buy financial assets, not residential real estate.[6]

It's important to note that these returns data are national averages, but real estate is both local and personal. Even though housing as an asset class has performed poorly, there are pockets of outperformance. Homeowners in parts of Brooklyn, Boston, and San Francisco, for example, have largely seen their properties appreciate. Whether or not those increases outperform the stock market depends on the particular property and many other factors. Home ownership can be a good investment, and some residential real estate does generate attractive returns, but across the United States, those outcomes are the exception, not the norm.

The Three Myths of Home Ownership

If the returns from residential real estate are low and owning too much house in your portfolio is risky, then why is there still such widespread demand to purchase a home? The answer is partly due to the persistent narrative about the financial benefits of home ownership. Many Americans accept the premise of home ownership as the foundation of the American Dream and default to that option without carefully considering the financial risks or evaluating other options.

The U.S. government has gone to great lengths at great cost to encourage home ownership through the mortgage interest deduction, interest deductions on home equity lines of credit, and favorable capital gains tax treatment of the sale of a primary residence. The American Dream narrative and these government policies rely on the unquestioning acceptance of the three common myths of home ownership.

MYTH #1: My home will appreciate in value.
Truth: Maybe, maybe not, depending on general economic conditions, your specific real estate market, the type of house you buy, the condition it's in, how well you maintain it, and where in the real estate cycle you buy and sell it.

MYTH #2: Owning "builds equity."
Truth: Relies on Myth #1. Ownership only builds equity if you buy a house that maintains or increases its value. You can make mortgage payments for a decade, but one sharp fall in the real estate market could put you in a position of negative equity, where the home is worth less than the remaining amount you owe on it.

You also only build equity if you hold the house for many years. The early years of mortgages are dominated by interest payments, not principal payments, so you build equity very slowly for more than a decade. If you buy a house through an interest-only loan, you don't build any equity at all by paying your mortgage.

MYTH #3: I can deduct mortgage interest payments on my taxes.

Truth: The majority of Americans aren't able to deduct mortgage interest on their taxes. The reason is that the mortgage interest deduction is only applied if you itemize deductions on your tax return, which, according to Tax Policy Center figures, only 30 percent of Americans do.[7] It only makes sense to itemize if your itemized deductions exceed the standard deduction (which in 2015 was $12,600 for a married couple filing jointly and $6,300 for a single person). For most Americans, the standard deduction will be higher than their itemized deductions, so they won't itemize. The Tax Policy Center reports that "The mortgage interest deduction (MID) provides the largest benefits in total and as a share of income to upper-middle-income taxpayers."[8]

The Real Costs of Owning a Home

Data on the mediocre returns from residential real estate may seem counterintuitive because you may have heard people (especially older generations) talk about the low prices they paid for their homes compared to the high prices they would sell for today. Those types of comparisons are flawed because they don't take into account inflation or incorporate the level of risk the buyer assumed, and they fail to include the total costs of the home.

There are a number of mortgage calculators online to help you assess the total cost of a home. According to the Federal Reserve, the median sales price for new homes sold in the United States at the end of 2015 was $297,000.[9] For ease of math, let's look at an example for a $300,000 home, as well as a $500,000 home for comparison. In our example, both have a fixed 30-year mortgage at a 4-percent interest rate, with a 10-percent down payment. At the end of 30 years, assuming you don't refinance or prepay, the total all-in, out-of-pocket cash costs of your $300,000 house will be $622,121, and the total cost of your $500,000 house will be more than $1 million dollars, or $1,031,867, to be exact.

Wait, what? How can a $500,000 house end up costing over a million dollars? Here's the math over 30 years (I used the mortgage calculator at mlcalc.com to run these numbers. In the table below, the assumptions I used are in parentheses, so you can rerun the calculation with different numbers).

TOTAL HOME PRICE VS. TOTAL HOME COST
10% down, 4% interest rate, 30-year fixed mortgage

$300,000 home		$500,000 home	
Down payment (10%)	$30,000	Down payment (10%)	$50,000
Principal	$270,000	Principal	$450,000
TOTAL HOME PRICE	$300,000	TOTAL HOME PRICE	$500,000
Interest (4%)	$194,048	Interest (4%)	$323,413
Property tax ($3,000/yr)*	$90,000	Property tax ($5,000/yr)*	$150,000
Home insurance ($1,000/yr)*	$30,000	Home insurance ($1,500/yr)*	$45,000
Mortgage insurance (until 2021)	$8,073	Mortgage insurance (until 2021)	$13,455
TOTAL HOME COST	$622,121	TOTAL HOME COST	$1,031,868

In this model, the property tax and insurance remained constant over the life of the mortgage. Therefore, the total home costs displayed here are understated. If we modeled realistic annual increases in taxes and insurance, the total cost would be higher. These figures also don't include any annual maintenance costs, or any cost of renovations, improvements, or upgrades during the 30 years. If we added these costs in, the total cost would be higher. Finally, these examples don't include the mortgage interest deduction.

These simplified examples illustrate that the total home cost, even without tax increases or ongoing maintenance or upgrades, is more than double the price the homeowner paid. And this is in a low-interest-rate environment. As recently as the mid-2000s, mortgage rates ranged from five to seven percent, compared to the recent three- to four-percent environment.

But What if I Really Want to Own a Home?

Home ownership is not always a bad financial idea, but for most middle-class Americans it is. The way middle-class Americans purchase houses (with too much debt) and own them (as too large a part of their portfolio), it's difficult to make a compelling case for home ownership. Many Americans also live in real estate markets with persistently low demand, stagnating or declining prices, and limited activity. When is home ownership a better financial idea? It can make sense if you purchase a house:

- ▶ With significant equity (a large down payment)
- ▶ With a small mortgage (meaning you buy smaller or buy later in life, when you're richer)
- ▶ As a small percentage of your overall assets and investment portfolio (meaning you buy smaller, later in life, or when you're richer)
- ▶ Located in an area with significant demand, like dense, urban, or near-urban areas, gentrifying neighborhoods, or destination locations (not the middle of Random Suburb, USA)

If you buy under these conditions, even if prices decline, you will be better positioned to weather the storm. The lessons from

2008 were clear: Too many Americans owned too much house financed by too much debt in unattractive real estate markets. If you're going to buy a house, steer clear of those mistakes.

Accessing a Home

There is some evidence that the access economy is growing for residential housing. The most recent research from Harvard's Joint Center on Housing Studies shows that 37 percent of U.S. households now rent, the highest level since the 1960s.[10] The number of households renting has grown more rapidly over this past decade (2005–2015) than any decade in the past 50 years. Renting has become more prevalent across all age groups, all income levels, and all household types. To evaluate the possibility (and financial impact) of renting, start with online calculators that can give you a preliminary idea of the financial differences between renting and buying both a home and a car.[11] Accessing housing instead of owning it might make more sense at various stages in your life.

If renting doesn't sound appealing, there is a new "Airbnb lifestyle" of accessing housing that might be more interesting. Returning ex-pats Elaine Kuok and David Roberts wrote about the year they spent living "home-free" in Airbnb apartments around New York City to explore a variety of neighborhoods.[12] Their lifestyle offers them flexibility they couldn't have if they were committed to a year-long lease or a multidecade mortgage. I contacted David on Twitter for an update, and, as of this writing, he and Elaine are enjoying a second year of their home-free lifestyle.

The market for accessing housing is young but is continuing to grow. WeWork, the company that offers coworking space for rent in major cities here and abroad, just launched its first We-Live property in New York City, with month-to-month rentals of fully furnished and decorated apartments. As demand for accessing housing increases, we can expect to see even more options emerge.

Diploma Debt

The second-largest expense Americans have is student loans. Buying an education and "owning" a diploma is expensive. Student loans have long been considered good debt because an investment in a college education pays off. Studies and statistics consistently show that college graduates earn more than non–college graduates over their lifetimes, which offers the most compelling support for the argument that college is an investment worth borrowing for.[13]

What's missing from the studies is the list of implicit assumptions that a strong case for borrowing must include: whether you attend a quality school, if you get a job after college (the unemployment and underemployment rates among college graduates are historically high[14]), and whether you earn a reasonable income relative to your debt levels (many graduates don't and name student loan repayments as their biggest expense, even above rent). Only when those conditions are met is there a strong argument for suggesting that taking out student loans is a sensible financial decision.

The Risk of Diploma Debt

Student loans might be "good debt," but they're also risky debt. The student loan lenders such as Sallie Mae used to take on meaningful repayment risk, as lenders normally should and do, but that risk has been mitigated by regulations that limit their exposure to defaults. For example, if the borrower falls behind in payments, government-backed student loan lenders have the right to garnish wages with just 30 days' notice and without a court order.[15] Contrary to popular opinion, student loans can be discharged through bankruptcy proceedings but only through a separate adversary proceeding. Only 0.1 percent of people with student debt apply for the proceeding when they file for bankruptcy.[16] The colleges themselves take no risk because their tuition is paid in advance each semester. That leaves the borrower as the only risk-taker in the student loan transaction.

Dealing with Diploma Debt

If you've already taken on student loan debt, then your choices for dealing with it are limited. You can refinance it to a lower interest rate, defer it, forbear it, apply for reduced payments, consolidate it, or spend the time and energy to pay it down as quickly as possible and move on with your life. How far down the road of fiscal parsimony you're willing to go to rid yourself of student loan debt depends on your goals and priorities and your tolerance for financial sacrifice. There are now numerous websites and blogs of graduates sharing their experiences and techniques for rapidly (usually in under a year) paying down their student loan debt. Joe Mihalic's website *No More Harvard Debt* is perhaps one of the better-known examples.[17]

On his site, Joe chronicled his quest to pay down $90,000 of business school debt in 10 months. He not only achieved this goal, he exceeded it. Joe was able to pay down his debt ahead of schedule, in just seven months, by cutting expenses, taking on side gigs, and selling and renting his stuff. Many of you will consider Joe's approach to be extreme, and it is, but it was also an effective and short-term strategy. If you feel as strongly about one of your own big, audacious goals, whether it's debt repayment or some other ambition, you might relate to being ferociously committed to accomplishing it and understand the willingness to do whatever it takes.

In an unexpected turn of events, there are early signs that employers are stepping in to relieve some of the financial burden of student loan debt. In 2016, companies like Fidelity, PricewaterhouseCoopers, and Natixis have piloted or introduced student loan repayment benefits in which they pay a fixed amount per year (at Fidelity it's $2,000) toward an employee's student loan balance.[18] Until it becomes much easier and more common to access credentials without owning a degree, this is a positive step toward reducing the financial burden of student loan debt on borrowers.

The college degree that used to land us in a well-paying, full-time corporate job can also terminate in a post-graduate life of debt, living in our parents' homes in our old bedrooms. We take a risk when we take on student loan debt, and regardless of the outcome, we still have to pay. Yet the data is clear that a college degree is the minimum requirement for many professional jobs. A college degree won't guarantee you better work and higher earnings, but it's likely to improve your odds.

Accessing Education

The Gig Economy is still in the early stages of a transition from a credentials-based economy of degrees, titles, and brand names to a skills-based economy that values specific knowledge and experience. Ivy League graduates and managing directors at Wall Street firms are still benefiting from the market-signaling effect of their degrees and titles, but the power of those credentials is waning in favor of workers with demonstrable experience and expertise.

We're seeing new ways of work emerge in which demonstrated skills, knowledge, and ratings from prior work experiences are what matter, not where you went to school or what degrees you have. Topcoder, Upwork, Freelancer, and 99designs are places to find work and build a reputation regardless of your degree and title-based credentials.

The premise behind these and other sites is that the work we do, the content we create, and results from skills and knowledge tests provide a more accurate assessment of skills and knowledge than a diploma or title. Ernst & Young in the United Kingdom conducted an internal study of 400 graduates and found no evidence correlating professional success with prior education, but they did find that strengths-based and numeric assessments were good indicators of whether a candidate would succeed at the firm. Based on the results, E&Y has removed academic criteria as a requirement for its entry-level positions.[19] It's an early and bold move away from the signaling effect of college grades and degrees. At most companies, assessments and tests are recruiting tools that supplement academic degrees and corporate titles, but we can imagine a day when they begin to supplant them.

ACCESS IS THE NEW OWNERSHIP

The U.S. economy depends heavily on consumer spending and demand. If the access economy continues to grow and increasingly replaces ownership, it will disrupt the national economy. If individuals increasingly access instead of own their houses and cars and accelerate their renting of consumer goods that they used to buy, the economic impact will be significant and widespread.

For individuals, the access economy is nothing short of a personal financial revolution. Imagine and evaluate the flexibility, variety, and cost savings you could potentially realize by access-ing consumer goods, cars, and housing. What would the impact be on your personal balance sheet? Ownership will still make sense in some cases and during some phases of life, but no longer needs to be the default choice. In a Gig Economy of insecure jobs and variable income, accessing the goods we want and need, without the debt, fixed costs, and physical ownership of so much stuff can be an attractive alternative.

To start thinking access, not ownership, consider:

- ▶ What would be the financial implications of accessing the biggest assets I own?
- ▶ Is home ownership for me, and what are the financial implications and costs of owning?
- ▶ Are there ways I can reduce my education debt?
- ▶ What opportunities are there for me to access education in the future?

Chapter Ten

SAVE FOR A TRADITIONAL RETIREMENT . . . BUT DON'T PLAN ON HAVING ONE

Yet there is no country and no people, I think, who can look forward to the age of leisure and of abundance without a dread.

—JOHN MAYNARD KEYNES

The elephant in the Gig Economy room is the question of when, and whether, we can ever stop working. If our working lives consist of multiple jobs and variable income, can we retire? The good news is that, yes, we can still retire. The Gig Economy retirement may never be the corporate-funded, work-free decades they once were, but there's a case to be made that with thoughtful planning and commitment, retirement can still exist.

The less-good news is that we have to save for and finance retirement ourselves. Corporate pensions are no longer around to foot the bill. Instead, employers have mass migrated to offering defined contribution retirement plans, such as 401(k)s, in which employees decide for themselves whether to participate in the plan, how much to contribute, and where to invest their contributions. Pensions still exist in the public sector for government workers and teachers but are generally underfunded, in some cases severely.[1] Government sources of retirement funds, like Social Security, appear unreliable at best and insolvent at worst, depending on your generation.

There are three discrete possibilities to retire in the Gig Economy:

- ▸ Save to finance a traditional retirement
- ▸ Plan to work longer and retire later
- ▸ Create a new vision of retirement

Let's look at each in turn.

Save to Finance a Traditional Retirement

Saving for retirement is a daunting task, but in the Gig Economy, independent workers have the opportunity to save more for retirement than a typical employee. Contractors and other independent workers who don't have access to a company-sponsored retirement plan can still save on their own through an Individual 401(k) or a SEP IRA.[2] Both options provide significantly higher contribution limits for independent workers—up to $53,000 per year—than employer-sponsored 401(k)s. The maximum employee contribution to an employer's 401(k) is $18,000 per year.

To illustrate with a simplified example, I used Vanguard's (simplified) online calculator to determine the eligible contributions of a contractor (sole proprietor) with $100,000 in net earnings.[3] That worker is eligible to contribute over $36,000 to her individual 401(k), compared to $18,000 for a similarly compensated employee participating in a company 401(k). Although employees are limited to contributing $18,000 to their 401(k)s, many employers offer a company match to supplement employees' contributions. In 2015, employers were allowed to contribute up to $35,000 to an employee's 401(k), but very few companies contribute anywhere near that amount. The average employer match is just 4.7 percent of employee salary.[4]

The opportunity to save more is even greater for more-highly-paid consultants and contractors. Using our simplified calculator, a contractor with net earnings of $185,000 is eligible to contribute the maximum $53,000 annually to retirement savings. The higher contribution limits make it easier for independent workers to "catch up" and save much more for retirement in their highest earning years and scale back in leaner times. This flexibility is better suited to the variable incomes that characterize the Gig Economy.

The table below summarizes how much more self-employed and contract workers are eligible to contribute to retirement accounts compared to employees.

Independent Workers Are Eligible to Save More for Retirement Annually than Employees

Plan	Eligible Participants	2015 Maximum Contribution*
Individual 401(k), also called Solo 401(k)	Self-employed/ partnership/ contractor/ freelancer	Up to $18,000 as an employee (plus another $6,000 if 50+ years old) *plus* up to 25 percent of net earnings as an employer, or $53,000, whichever is less
SEP IRA	Self-employed/ partnership/ contractor/ freelancer	25 percent of compensation or $53,000, whichever is less
401(k)/403(b)/527, etc.	Employee/ Employer	*Employee:* $18,000 (plus another $6,000 if 50+ years old); *Employer:* $35,000 or 100 percent of employee salary, whichever is less*
Traditional or Roth IRA	Employee and/or self-employed/ contractor/ freelancer	$5,500 (plus another $1,000 if 50+ years old)*

* For specific definitions and calculations, see www.irs.gov/pub/irs-pdf/p560. pdf and www.irs.gov/Retirement-Plans/One-Participant-401(k)-Plans

All workers, both employees and contractors, can *also* contribute to an IRA, up to a limit of $5,500 for those under age 50 and $6,500 for those over age 50.[5] In theory, then, a well-paid contractor could contribute $58,500 annually to retirement accounts—a maximum $53,000 to an Individual 401(k) and another $5,500 to a traditional or Roth IRA. This compares to $23,000 a company employee could contribute to a 401(k) ($18,000) and an IRA ($5,500).

Of course, there's a big difference between having the opportunity to save and actually saving. Therein lies the crux of the problem for both Gig Economy workers and traditional employees, both of whom have a persistent tendency to not save, regardless of the opportunity to do so.

Americans on average aren't good savers.[6] We have a very low savings rate as a nation, and it trends even lower when it comes to saving for retirement. This trend is understandable for lower-income workers whose ability to save is limited, but in fact our poor savings behavior is persistent across income ranges. Economist Allison Schrager has written about what she calls "high-earning poor people."[7] She analyzed Federal Reserve data and found that upper-middle-class workers age 40 to 55 with annual incomes $75,000 to $100,000 have, on average, less than one year's salary saved for retirement. They reported an average of just $70,000 in retirement savings. In that same income range, a full one-quarter of individuals had saved less than $17,500.

Most Americans (54 percent) have less than $25,000 in retirement savings and investments.[8] Some studies of middle-class Americans place that number even lower, at a median of $20,000.[9]

Those amounts are nowhere near enough to cover any kind of retirement. Estimates on how much retirees need to just cover healthcare costs are multiples of what most Americans have saved. A couple with "average income" should expect healthcare costs in retirement of about $266,000.[10] Adding in dental, vision, and hearing costs brings the total to $395,000, and that still doesn't include long-term care or the amounts needed to cover general living expenses.

This lack of retirement savings is not just a Gig Economy problem. Companies have shifted the risk, and burden, of saving for retirement to employees, but employees simply aren't saving sufficiently. About half of private-sector workers in traditional full-time jobs have access to a 401(k) or another retirement plan at work. On average, over 60 percent of employees (this percentage varies by age, income, and size of company) choose to participate in them, but they still don't save enough to replace just one year of their current income during retirement.[11] Even when they have access to a company retirement plan that offers them automatic savings through payroll deductions *and* matching employer contributions, workers don't contribute very much to them. Employees choose to invest, on average, just 5 to 7 percent of their salary, and many employees don't contribute enough to take full advantage of the employer match.[12] Surveys by both Vanguard and Wells Fargo have found that the median 401(k) balances hover around $30,000.[13]

The takeaway from all this data is that those of us who plan to retire must plan to finance it ourselves, and the best way to do so is to save through at least two vehicles: an IRA *and* either a 401(k) or SEP IRA. We also have to do a better job of actually saving. The prior two chapters offer suggestions for increasing our financial flexibility, as well as reducing the amount of money we tie up in owning, and servicing the debt to own, large assets. Following are three more suggestions about how to increase retirement savings.

Increase savings by saving automatically: If you want to be a better saver, stop procrastinating and set up an automatic savings plan (like direct deposit) so you don't have to think about it. Researchers from Stanford and the University of Minnesota have found that procrastination (which they refer to as "present-biased preferences") causes individuals to make plans in the present but delay actions until the future.[14] Policymakers have suggested automatic enrollment in retirement savings plans as a way to overcome this issue, and in fact participation rates in automatic enrollment plans are about 10 percent higher than optional enrollment plans (77 percent vs. 68 percent of those eligible).[15]

Increase savings by picking the right time horizon: Look ahead and think long term to motivate saving for retirement. We saw in chapter 1 that selecting the right time horizon can help us achieve our goals. Research from the Social Security Administration shows that workers who have a short time horizon (e.g., the next few months, next year) are less likely to save for retirement than those planning with longer time horizons in mind (e.g., the next 5 to 10 years).

Increase savings by developing a financial plan: We discussed in chapter 8 how having a financial plan creates a framework to help us achieve our financial goals. It can also help us save. Research conducted by the Certified Financial Planner (CFP) Board and the Consumer Federation of America found that households that did even basic financial planning had a significant increase in retirement planning and savings.[16]

The need to save for retirement is a recent phenomenon. Americans age 65 and older, known as the Great Generation, have amassed significant wealth and have been the "greatest economic gainers in this century," according to a recent Pew report.[17] They are the last generation that will enjoy the guaranteed trifecta of corporate pensions, fully funded Social Security, and Medicare to fund a comfortable and secure retirement. This generation also benefited from a persistent increase in real estate prices that created wealth and introduced financial flexibility into their lives. The beneficiaries of this economic largesse should be the current generation of older workers, the Baby Boomers, who are just now retiring. A recent report by Accenture found that a Great Transfer of over $12 trillion is currently passing from the Great Generation to the Baby Boomers and will supplement their retirement.[18]

But there's an even Greater Transfer of $30 trillion that Baby Boomers will hand down to Generation X starting in 2031. Gen X is the first generation that will rely mostly on their own savings to fund retirement. They missed the era of funded corporate pensions and are the first generation to have to wait until age 67 to receive full Social Security benefits. This peak transfer could provide a just-in-time financial cushion to this under-resourced generation. Unfortunately, estimates suggest that it will only be a small cushion, not a silver bullet that secures Gen X's retirement. Today's seniors are living longer—85+ is one of the fastest-growing age brackets in the United States—which means that they spend more of their assets during their lives and incur significant healthcare expenses, both of which limit the capital they have available to hand down to future generations.[19] For Gen X and later generations, saving is the best and most secure way to plan for retirement.

Plan to Work Longer and Retire Later

Many workers believe that if they don't have sufficient retirement savings, they can just work longer, earn more money, and retire later. More than one-third (37 percent) of workers expect to retire after age 65, compared to 11 percent in 1991.[20] More than half of workers age 40+ plan to work into their 70s because they won't have enough retirement savings to live comfortably.[21]

Fortunately, the Gig Economy offers retirees more opportunities to work. Granny might not be able to hold a full-time corporate job into her 70s, but now there are many other options for her to work part time, at home, and on her own schedule. She can dog sit on Rover.com, host dinners for paying diners through Feastly or EatWith, or rent a room of her house on Airbnb. She can work remotely on administrative or other small tasks on Upwork or as an Amazon Mechanical Turk. She can drive for Uber a few hours a week or babysit through Care.com. In the Gig Economy, retirees looking to supplement Social Security or an underfunded IRA can more easily than ever find flexible (and even home-based) work to generate incremental income.

Even with more options for flexible work, planning to work longer is a risky plan because we don't fully control when we'll stop working. Unanticipated health or disability can and do force older workers to stop working earlier than they planned. Recent surveys found that nearly one-half (46 percent) of retirees leave the workforce earlier than they planned and that the majority of those (55 percent) leave involuntarily because of health or disability issues.[22] The director of one of the surveys noted that:

> Half the retirees in this study retired earlier than expected for reasons beyond their control. People who think working longer—perhaps into their 70s or later—is a retirement plan should realize they may not be able to work longer. Unforeseen circumstances crop up, and this is really important for people to recognize.[23]

Retiring earlier than planned due to health problems is

double trouble because we lose working income we had projected and healthcare costs surge. Companies used to bear the risk of retiree healthcare costs by providing private insurance that supplemented Medicare, but not anymore. Today, less than one-quarter (23 percent) of companies offer retiree health benefits.[24] Health problems or disability can also limit our ability to generate even incremental income through flexible or home-based work.

Working longer before retiring is a possibility but not something we can reliably plan. It gives us the option to generate supplemental income during retirement, not survive it.

Create a New Vision of Retirement

Many people still think of traditional retirement and imagine a sun-drenched, blissed-out end to working life: leisurely days of golf, swimming, grandchildren, and cocktail hours that start in the afternoon. That kind of retirement can still exist if it's what we want and if we're willing to save for it. There are many other versions and visions of retirement, though, and it's my hope that the exercises in this book that helped you articulate your priorities, understand your spending, and plan across multiple time horizons will also help you craft and create your ideal retirement.

In the Gig Economy, retirement is less of an end to our working lives and the beginning of leisure than it is a continuation of the mix of work and leisure we've had all along. It's a more fluid, and arguably more balanced, way to live. In the Gig Economy, our working lives are interspersed with periods of "mini-retirement," and our "retirement" is intermingled with time spent working.[25] We can use time between gigs and between jobs to pursue goals that prior generations deferred until retirement. We can travel, golf, live by a beach, and spend chunks of quality time with our family during breaks in our careers, not just at the end. We can also develop side gigs to develop our interests and passions during our working years— activities that we can then carry over into our retirement years.

It's a bit too early in the Gig Economy for there to be many examples of how workers have envisioned and taken retirement. In the meantime, today's retirees can be a source of inspiration and ideas about how to create an interesting, fun, active, and meaningful retirement. Type the words *retiree*, *blog*, and *adventure* into Google and settle in for some reading about seniors who are engaging in service and volunteer work, traveling the United States by RV, Airbnb-ing their way around Europe, or writing about cultural life and activities in their city. Developing specific ideas now for what your ideal version of retirement looks like is a useful exercise. Creating a vision will help you estimate how much it's likely to cost and help motivate you to save enough to realize it.

Succeeding in the Gig Economy requires different skills than succeeding as an employee. If you've cultivated those skills—developing an opportunity mindset, diversifying your work, taking time between gigs, and becoming financially flexible—then you'll have all the tools you need to create your own customized plan for the end of your working life.

SAVING IS THE NEW PENSION

Employers and the government have successfully pushed the risk and burden of funding retirement almost completely onto workers, and there are no signs of that reversing. Workers now have to rely on a mix of their own savings, continuing to work in some capacity for as long as possible, and creatively planning for their own version of retirement.

As you think about preparing for retirement, consider:

▶ How much can I save for retirement each year?

▶ What can I do to become a better saver for my retirement?

▶ How can I use all the rules and tools in this book to help
me craft my own customized version of retirement?

THE FUTURE GIG ECONOMY

My father had one job in his lifetime, I will have six jobs in my lifetime, and my children will have six jobs at the same time.

—ROBIN CHASE, FOUNDER OF ZIPCAR

Our perceptions about work are formed at a very young age. From the time we're kids, adults ask us what we want to be when we grow up, and the answers reflect what we see around us— employees in full-time jobs. We answer that we want to be teachers or doctors or firefighters. I haven't yet heard a kid say that she wants to be a consultant, or a freelancer, or a contractor. But if I did, that's the one I'd bet on, because that kid understands that employees in full-time jobs aren't the future of work. By the time today's kids grow up, becoming an employee and getting a full-time job will be the exception, not the rule.

The Employee vs. Contractor Debate

The Gig Economy is still emerging and gaining traction. Along the way, it's exposing our obsolete, outdated, and confusing labor market policies. There has been much debate about how to change our laws and modify our labor markets in response to the Gig Economy. The most important and significant one centers on how to address the current categorization of workers as either employees or contractors.

The distinction between contractor and employee is vague and variable but the cost difference to employers is considerable and clear. Full-time employees are estimated to be 30–40 percent more costly than contractors due to the added costs of taxes, insurance, and benefits.[1] Companies with full-time employees are required to pay federal income, Social Security, and Medicare taxes for each employee, as well as federal and state unemployment taxes and workers' compensation. Some businesses are also required to provide Family Medical Leave (if they have more than 50 employees), and most companies pay the costs of voluntary benefits, including paid time off, access to health, disability and life insurance, and a 401(k) match. Companies aren't required to offer these benefits, but many do.

Our labor market policies force companies to offer work structured around rigid categories—employee vs. contractor—rather than allowing them to more precisely allocate labor to meet their business needs. Not unexpectedly, employers are actively arbitraging the cost disparity between the two types of workers. Many companies are reducing their number of employees and hiring more contractors, or even misclassifying workers, in order to realize lower labor costs.[2] Even if companies would prefer more full-time, dedicated staff, our labor market policies provide incentives to hire more short-term, cheaper, contract labor than they otherwise would.

For workers, policies that differentiate between employees and contractors create an economic "winner takes all" paradigm where, if you're a full-time employee, you pay lower taxes and have access to a discounted package of employer-provided benefits and protections only available to workers in traditional jobs. Contractors, on the other hand, pay both employer and employee taxes on their earnings, and must attempt to purchase their own benefits on the private market, at much higher rates. Under our current labor market structure, workers are disproportionately better off if they're full-time employees.

This sharp economic divide between employee and contractor leads to excess demand for full-time jobs. It encourages workers to seek traditional, full-time, benefit-rich jobs, even if they would prefer less than full-time hours and be willing to take lower compensation in exchange. It also drives employers to seek and hire any labor *except* full-time employees, even if they would ideally prefer the dedicated attention of an employee that they could control and manage.

The demarcation between employees and contractors introduces a "kink" in the labor market that creates permanent distortions and inefficiencies. Changing status from contractor to employee *disproportionately* increases costs to businesses and compensation to employees. The forced categorization of workers compels businesses to limit labor hours and the supply of full-time jobs and encourages workers who would prefer to work less to increase their demand for full-time work. This artificial divide between employees and contractors doesn't optimize the preferences of either buyers or sellers of labor and creates a labor market that is in persistent disequilibrium.

So far, the Department of Labor has not expressed an interest or willingness to quantify the size and growth of the Gig Economy through data collection, or enact any policy changes to support it. The government has stood inactively by, failing to update policies to offer increased security and financial stability to workers who don't hold a full-time corporate job. It has stuck stubbornly to an old, outdated model that defines "jobs" and "employees" in ways that are increasingly irrelevant and obstruct innovation, growth, and opportunity.

This old model is as confusing as it is outdated. The current definitions of employee and contractor are vague, qualitative, and vary among several different agencies. For example, the IRS provides a list of factors to help identify an employee versus a contractor, but the factors on the list are not easily quantified, weighted, or prioritized.[3] The Department of Labor has issued an entirely different but equally subjective list of factors in its "administrator's interpretation" of who is an employee and who is a contractor.[4] The National Labor Relations Board (NLRB) has issued yet another list that it applies and weights on a case-by-case basis.[5]

The government's unwillingness to promulgate one set of clear definitions for employee and contractor shifts the risk of incorrectly classifying workers onto both companies and the workers themselves. The confusion and opacity around how to define each category and differentiate between the two has led to costly legal battles about how workers are classified, requires companies to take on regulatory and legal risk, and places workers in an uncertain position with employers.

What will spur the government into action to update these antiquated labor market policies is anybody's guess. What is clear is that the government enjoys some economic benefits of maintaining the status quo of our current employment market. As collector of tax revenues, the government prefers that there be more employees. Since companies are responsible for reporting and collecting taxes on behalf of their employees, the government sees a 99-percent tax compliance rate from employers, for income, Social Security, and Medicare taxes. If a worker switches categories and becomes a contractor, tax reporting and compliance drop to less than half (about 44 percent).[6] If the government implements policy changes that support the rise of independent work and acknowledges the decline of the employee, the result will almost certainly be lower tax revenues. In 2015, payroll taxes represented 33 percent of tax dollars raised, a meaningful percentage of the government's inflows.[7]

Government inaction and unwillingness to update labor policies is causing confusion, distorting the labor market, and forcing companies and workers to take on risk when they opt to work outside of the rigid constructs of a full-time job. Until government labor policies change, workers will continue to have no way to access certain benefits, rights, and protections unless they have a traditional job, and companies will continue to have both the opportunity and economic incentive to hire contractors instead of employees.

What the Future Gig Economy Might Look Like

The debate about what the future Gig Economy will look like has generated new proposals about how to reform and restructure our labor market. The following proposals represent a subset that have gained traction in the debate. They give us some early ideas about how the Gig Economy might evolve going forward.

Eliminate Categorization of Workers

First to go would most certainly be the complicated, ill-defined, and outdated distinctions between employee and contractor. A change in policy that removes this artificial "kink" in the market would eliminate the resulting inefficiencies and economic distortions that provide incentives for employers to arbitrage among categories of workers. Instead of hiring contractors because they're so much cheaper than employees, an employer could just hire *workers* for however many hours they are needed.[8]

If we allowed companies to more fluidly pay workers along a continuum rather than navigate and choose between discrete categories, both companies and workers could be better off.

Companies could offer work structured entirely around the actual demands of their businesses, and workers could offer their labor based entirely on their specific preferences for work and income. If businesses could pay workers based on hours worked, it would create a liquid and more efficient labor market. It would eliminate the inefficiencies, perverse incentives, and arbitraging that the artificial classifications of our current labor system encourage.

Add a Third Category of Worker

Instead of eliminating worker categorization, one of the most common, incremental policy proposals for the Gig Economy is to add another one.[9] Numerous academics and policy commentators propose creating a new third legal category of "independent worker" or "dependent contractor" as an intermediate category between employee and contractor. This third category of worker would get some but not all of the protections offered to traditional employees. This third option has already been tested and proven in Canada, Germany, and Spain. This proposal is incremental in that it simply augments our existing categorization system and maintains employers' ability to arbitrage among categories.

Offer Prorated and Portable Benefits

Financial planner Michael Kitces sees a world where most workplaces no longer provide employee benefits. Instead, employers would allocate the money previously used for benefits directly to the employees as part of their salary or compensation. Employees then decide and select what benefits to purchase. In Kitces's words, "After all, what's the difference between an employer paying $50,000/year, plus $500/month for health insurance and a 3 percent contribution ($1,500) to a retirement plan, versus simply paying the employee $57,500 in salary and letting the employee make the decisions?"[10] This proposal is administratively simple but relies on either private or government-assisted marketplaces (like the health exchanges under the Affordable Care Act) to provide individuals a way to select and purchase affordable benefits.

Most other proposals are more administratively complex and involve an intermediary to manage the purchase of benefits. David Rolf and Nick Hanauer propose the proration, portability, and universality of benefits. With proration, the accrual of benefits is based on hours worked. If someone works 30 hours per week (out of a standard 40-hour work week), she should get three-quarters of full-time benefits from her place of work. Universality ensures that a basic set of benefits and labor standards must be standard across "all employers and all forms of employment." This way, the difference in benefits between employees and contractors would become less pronounced. To ensure portability, the authors propose that these benefits are accrued via automatic payroll deductions and pooled into what they call a Shared Security Account, administered by a third party.[11]

Steven Hill, a senior fellow at the New America Foundation and author of *Raw Deal: How the "Uber" Economy and Runaway Capitalism are Screwing American Workers* proposes a similar multiemployer plan that requires all employers to pay benefits to workers based on either hours worked or gross wages. The benefits payments would go into an Individual Security Account and then pay, via payroll deductions, into Social Security, Medicare, and unemployment.[12]

Create Wage Insurance

Former Labor Secretary Robert Reich and public policy professor Robert LaLonde both advocate for a form of income insurance that protects independent workers from declines in income. The mechanics of the different proposals vary, but the idea is to reduce the volatility of the Gig Economy's variable income. Income insurance could either supplement or replace unemployment insurance. In Reich's example, if "your monthly income dips more than 50 percent below the average monthly income you've received from all the jobs you've taken over the preceding five years, you'd automatically receive half the difference for up to a year."[13]

Implement a Universal Basic Income

Robert Reich and others have publicly come out in support of a universal basic income (UBI), or basic income guarantee.[14] UBI is a guaranteed, fixed amount paid by the government to every citizen for life, regardless of employment or work status. In turn, governments eliminate public assistance and poverty programs such as unemployment and food assistance. UBI has not been implemented in any other country, so there is no empirical evidence about its effects and consequences.

A twist on the UBI proposal is offered by British economist Tim Harford. He goes beyond suggesting that the government guarantee only income and proposes that the government provide healthcare, pensions, and income to everyone, at a very basic level. Anything above the state-provided "safety net" must be paid for by individuals themselves or by employers who provide them voluntarily. He calls his proposal "libertarianism with a safety net."[15]

Allow Contractors to Collectively Bargain

The National Labor Relations Act applies only to employees, thus excluding independent contractors from the ability to bargain collectively. In the past, contractor attempts to unionize and bargain have been thwarted by invoking antitrust laws. The argument is that contractors who collectively bargain to set common rates are essentially colluding, which violates antitrust laws. However, in December 2015, the Seattle City Council voted to extend collective bargaining rights to Uber and Lyft drivers.[16] In March, the U.S. Chamber of Commerce sued the city of Seattle, saying that the ordinance violates antitrust laws.[17] California is expected to introduce a similar bill covering independent contractors who work on on-demand platforms.

What most of these proposals have in common is that they attempt to improve the current labor market by eliminating an employer's ability to arbitrage between employees and contractors, and support worker choices about how to work. Their overarching goal is to allow workers in the Gig Economy to be able to access benefits and protections that are similar to what employees currently receive.

The Future of 'Good Jobs'

The growth of the Gig Economy has raised concerns that it is eliminating "good jobs," which are required for a prosperous economy and a healthy middle class. As we discussed in the introduction, "bad jobs" are easy to spot because we all have a sense of what those are. They are jobs with low pay, few or no benefits, and low levels of autonomy, control, and meaning. Bad jobs are persistent in our current economy and the Gig Economy doesn't make them go away. What it does do is create the opportunity to turn those bad jobs into better work, which is a step in the right direction.

Good jobs, on the other hand, are more difficult to identify. There are many ways to think about what constitutes a good job.

- ► Gallup defines a good job as "one with 30+ hours of work a week with a consistent paycheck from an employer. A *great* job is a job in which you believe your boss cares about your development, you can use your individual strengths at work, and you believe your work makes a contribution to something."[18]
- ► According to Zeynep Ton, an MIT professor and author of *The Good Jobs Strategy*, a good job is one "with decent pay, decent benefits, and stable work schedules" and where "employees can perform well and find meaning and dignity in their work."[19]
- ► Author Steven Hill says that a good job is one that provides "decent pay, healthcare, retirement, a safety net, with a measure of job security."[20]

These differing perspectives highlight the difficulty of defining what a "good job" really is. We can all agree that every worker wants to be paid well, but even what 'well' is varies tremendously. Not everyone puts compensation at the top of their list of what matters. There are plenty of workers who choose to take lower paying jobs over other, more lucrative options. Talk to just about anyone in the nonprofit world, in a public sector job, or aspiring to be an actor or artist, and discover why compensation isn't most important. There are also many other workers who are willing to trade compensation for other job benefits, such as reduced hours, flexibility, or more time off. Some base level of compensation is clearly important, but we can't precisely identify what it is, or what economics make for a good job.

At its core, a good job, like beauty, is in the eye of the beholder. Worker expectations matter in any assessment of what a good job is. One person's dream job is another's version of a Dilbert cartoon. Some people want work to challenge and absorb them. They derive a sense of *Flow*, or deep enjoyment and creativity, from their days and look for a job that provides that feeling.[21] Others want to go to work and then leave it completely behind at the end of the day.

Even if we wanted more good jobs—however we define them—the reality is that jobs are becoming more scarce. Full-time job creation has been declining over the past decade and is at historic lows. Employees are an expensive and inflexible source of labor. Corporations are automating tasks, outsourcing, and contracting out work in order to avoid hiring full-time employees, who have become the worker of last resort. These trends suggest that we won't sustain the middle class by clinging to the old employee-in-a-job model. Instead, we're left to consider a different foundation for the middle class that is realistic and sustainable in the Gig Economy.

The traditional economic foundation of the middle class is already crumbling because it was built on the expectation of—no, the *reliance on*—steady and long-term income from secure full-time jobs. Now that no job—no matter how you define it—is secure, any lifestyle built upon the assumption of a steady, uninterrupted flow of income is risky at best, delusional at worst. Any prudent economic plan has to include the probability that income will vary, and jobs will change. The middle class will have to be rebuilt on a different foundation in the Gig Economy.

Traditional Work Foundation	Gig Economy Foundation
Steady paychecks	Diversified income
Secure full-time jobs	Work, not jobs
Highly leveraged home ownership	Low leverage or no leverage flexible living arrangements
Corporate-financed retirement	Individual savings for retirement and ongoing time off between gigs

This new foundation of the middle class is smaller. It won't support the heavy weight of debt and consumption that characterized the old middle class lifestyle. As we enter a work world that doesn't offer a long-term reliable income or any sense of job security, we should expect to see workers choosing a far less leveraged, more variable cost lifestyle because they don't know what the future holds.

The highly leveraged, high-overhead middle-class lifestyle simply isn't sustainable in the Gig Economy

The Future of Work: Stop Looking for a Job

As we've seen throughout this book, we can, through a portfolio of diverse work, and independent of a full-time job, achieve decent pay, access good benefits, including our own healthcare coverage and retirement savings, have autonomy and control, pursue work that we believe is meaningful, and structure a life that is consistent with our vision of success and our priorities. In the Gig Economy, we can simply remove the rigid framework of a *job* and instead talk about how to encourage an economy of *good work*, no matter how it is organized and structured. We can achieve the benefits of a good job without having to get a job.

This finding has enormous implications for workers, employers, and our economy. If we can accept that the future of work is based on work, not jobs, then we can start changing policies to give workers benefits, protections, and rights no matter how much or how they work. We can close the enormous loophole that allows (and provides incentives for) companies to avoid paying taxes and benefits for workers who aren't employees. And we can stop focusing on "job creation" as a policy goal and instead focus on "work creation." We can advocate for policies that encourage and support workers to work however they choose: in jobs, as a contractor, by the project, or on-demand.

Our labor market needs to reflect that work in the Gig Economy doesn't always, or even mostly, take place in a job. We no longer have to work for a single employer, in a prestructured, predefined, rigidly organized job, to obtain the benefits of a *good job*. In the Gig Economy, we can stop looking for a good job, and focus instead on finding good work.

Independent workers are still a small slice of today's workforce, but the Gig Economy is growing rapidly. Today's kids will still grow up in world dominated by full-time employees. Tomorrow's kids are likely to enter a workforce where fewer and fewer people are full-time employees in full-time jobs. Having a diverse portfolio of work will be the new normal, and being a full-time employee for a single employer the exception.

When we ask kids of the future what they want to be when they grow up they won't have an answer.

They'll have a list.

ACKNOWLEDGMENTS

It took the Gig Economy to write this book. My working life in the Gig Economy inspired it, the MBA class I teach on the topic informed it, and a whole team of independent Gig Economy workers helped research, edit, and review the manuscript, transcribed interviews, built a website, crafted a social media strategy, and agreed to be interviewed. As a team, we didn't organize one conference call or attend one meeting, and none of our work took place in a cubicle (or even in an office). For those reasons alone, we all want the Gig Economy to be the future of work.

So, first thanks go to the team. I was beyond lucky when I found Emily Adams as my research assistant. She joined me in the early stages of drafting this book, and stayed with me until the last submission, researching articles and reports, editing drafts, talking through concepts and ideas, and in the midst of it all, undergoing her own transformation from full-time employee to working independently in the Gig Economy. I am incredibly grateful and appreciative for the many significant contributions she made to this book.

I thank all of the many people I interviewed about the topics in this book. I appreciate their willingness to share their experiences, perspectives, and stories about their personal and professional lives in the Gig Economy. I especially thank those that have also been willing to speak in my class, including Sharon Bially, Dorie Clark, Devin Cole, Jessica Fox, Rachel

Greenberger, Deanna Jacobsen, Yoon Lee, Shannon O'Brien, Laura Gassner Otting, Beth Rogers, Allison Shapira, Gail Simmons, and Michelle Toth.

I want to thank my research assistant Caitria O'Neill, for making early contributions to this book and then validating the ideas in it by heading off to successfully create and live her own Gig Economy life. Many thanks go to Deanna Jacobsen for creating and executing social media for all my writing, for my website, and for speaking in my class as a social media expert. I am so grateful to Lauren Paap, whose incredibly intuitive work provided me with balance and energy during the entire writing of this book. Upwork has been a great source of transcribers, as well as manuscript editors and reviewers. I want to give special thanks to editors Josh Raab and Karen Best for their careful and helpful reviews of my manuscript during early submissions.

I'm also lucky to have good friends who agreed to read and review early drafts. Huge thanks to Sharon Bially for valuable feedback and edits on the proposal for this book, the manuscript, and for advice and help on all things PR. The same huge thanks to Jill Simeone for reading every manuscript I've ever written, and for the excellent insights and edits that always make them better. Cherone Duggan and I had many long chats about work and life in the Gig Economy that were valuable in solidifying the ideas in this book. Many thanks also go to Cherone for reading and providing edits on early drafts of the manuscript, and to Caitlin Lewis and Megan Prasad for reading and commenting on several chapters.

My colleagues at Babson College have given me an academic home and a wonderful teaching environment for the past six years. I created the idea and the syllabus for my Gig Economy class in 2011, before the term "Gig Economy" was part of the popular lexicon, and right from the first draft, Dr. Candy Brush provided enormous support and encouragement for the idea.

Candy has been a champion, a supporter, and a mentor during my entire tenure at Babson, and I couldn't be more grateful. Len Schlesinger, the President of Babson, was an equally early and enthusiastic evangelist for the Gig Economy, and championed my course at every opportunity. I'm very lucky to have colleagues like Amy Blitz, Susan Duffy, Patti Greene, Rachel Greenberger, and Jan Shubert, who have offered support, counsel, and friendship.

Over the past five years of teaching the Gig Economy in Babson's MBA program, my students have given me excellent feedback, asked insightful questions, challenged my assertions, and generously shared their own experiences, perspectives, and opinions about the changes they see and face in the workforce. I thank them all.

The Ewing Marion Kauffman Foundation has been my professional home for the past six years, and my colleagues there continue to provide tremendous support and counsel for all my writing endeavors. My fellow Fellows at the Foundation, Diana Kander and Alicia Robb, as well as my colleagues Alana Muller and Allison Schrager have been particularly helpful to the research and writing of this book.

Both my professional and writing lives have been encouraged, supported, and pushed (when needed) by my incredible mentor, Harold Bradley. We are an unlikely pairing, and I'll never really understand the whole baseball thing, but he has brought out my best work, helped me become a better writer, and taught me everything I know about being a gadfly.

New York City has been my publishing home for this book. Many thanks go to Alexandra Machinist at Janklow & Nesbit for originally signing me on, and to Paul Lucas for becoming my agent after she left, and guiding me expertly through the process of selling and publishing this book. Special thanks also go to Michael Steger at Janklow & Nesbit for his excellent, patient, and helpful legal work.

I'm a lucky author to work with AMACOM. Highest praise goes to my editor, Ellen Kadin, for her encouragement, patience, and early belief in this book and the ideas in it. Barry Richardson gave me incredibly helpful comments on the first submission of this manuscript, and the book is much improved thanks to his review. I also thank Jenny Wesselmann and Irene Majuk at AMACOM for their help with sales and marketing.

My actual home is both in Boston and in Dublin. My parents and my in-laws provide ongoing love, support, and much appreciated opportunities to relax over home-cooked meals. My brother, and my brothers- and sisters-in-law, are both friends and family to me, and provide love, support, and much appreciated opportunities to relax and hang out over glass(es) of wine. I have the best nieces, and the most fun visits and sleepovers with them. Much love goes to Devyn, Heather, Julia, Margot, Rachel, Ruth, Sophie, and Taylor.

We have the family we're born into, and the ones we choose. It was the best decision we made to join the Harvard Host Family program and become a host family to Cherone Duggan, Kasey LeBlanc, Caitlin Lewis, Yuying Luo, Megan Prasad, and Amy Stockton. Lots of #HostFam love to each of them.

Our house is a home thanks to our wonderful neighborhood and neighbors. Many thanks to our street, especially #14, #8, #6, #4, and the Murphys. Boston's writing community is a special one and I'm very happy to have been a member of the fabulous Grub Street for the past several years, as well as the Boston Writer's Room.

The most heartfelt thanks go to my husband Kevin, to whom this book is dedicated, for the love, the adventure, and for the most fun and interesting life I could imagine.

NOTES

INTRODUCTION

1. Bureau of Labor Statistics, Employee Tenure Summary, September 18, 2014. www.bls.gov/news.release/tenure.nr0.htm
2. Gould, Elise, Economic Policy Institute, "2014 continues a 35-year trend of broad-base wage stagnation," February 19, 2015. www.epi.org/publication/stagnant-wages-in-2014/
3. Adkins, Amy, "Majority of U.S. Employees Not Engaged Despite Gains in 2014," *Gallup*, January 28, 2015, www.gallup .com/poll/181289/majority-employees-not-engaged-despite-gains-2014.aspx
4. The Conference Board, "Surge in Hiring Lifts Outlook for Workers But Overall Job Satisfaction Remains Below 50%," September 8, 2015. www.conference-board.org/press/pressdetail. cfm?pressid=5545
5. Freelancers Union, Freelancing in America: 2015, An independent study commissioned by the Freelancers Union and Upwork. Also, Rasch, Rena, "Your Best Workers May Not Be Your Employees: A Global Study of Independent Workers," IBM Smarter Work-force Institute, October 2014. public.dhe.ibm. com/common/ssi/ecm/lo/en/lol14027usen/LOL14027USEN. PDF? Also see Field Nation, The New Face of the American Workforce, 2014. info.fieldnation.com/new-face-of-the-american-workforceamerica-vacation-workaholic-culture-labor-day
6. PriceWaterhouseCoopers, "Work-Life 3.0: Understanding How We'll Work Next, 2016. www.pwc.com/us/en/industry/ entertainment-media/publications/consumer-intelligence-series/ assets/pwc-consumer-intellgience-series-future-of-work-june-2016.pdf. See Also, Freelancers Union, Freelancing in America: 2015. fu-web-storage-prod.s3.amazonaws.com/content/filer_ public/59/e7/59e70be1-5730-4db8-919f-1d9b5024f939/survey_ 2015.pdf

7. Mills, Karen, G., "Growth & Shared Prosperity," Harvard Business School, U.S. Competitiveness Project. www.hbs .edu/competitiveness/Documents/growth-and-shared-prosperity.pdf

8. Haltiwanger, John, Ron S. Jarmin, and Javier Miranda, "Who Creates Jobs? Small Versus Large Versus Young," *The Review of Economics and Statistics*, May 2013. www.mitpressjournals .org/doi/pdf/10.1162/REST_a_00288

9. Ewing Marion Kauffman Foundation, The Importance of Young Firms for Economic Growth, Entrepreneurship Policy Digest, updated September 14, 2015. www.kauffman.org/~/media/ kauffman_org/resources/2014/entrepreneurship%20policy%20 digest/september%202014/entrepreneurship_policy_digest_ september2014.pdf

10. Reedy, E. J., and Robert E. Litan, "Starting Smaller; Staying Smaller: America's Slow Leak in Job Creation," Ewing Marion Kauffman Foundation, July 2011. www.kauffman.org/~/media/ kauffman_org/research%20reports%20and%20covers/2011/07/ job_leaks_starting_smaller_study.pdf

11. U.S. Senate Committee on Health, Education, Labor, and Pensions, U.S. Department of Labor, "Statement of Seth D. Harris Deputy Secretary U.S. Department of Labor Before the Committee on Health, Education, Labor, and Pensions," June 17, 2010.

12. Department of Labor, "$10.2m awarded to fund worker misclassification detection, enforcement activities in 19 state unemployment insurance programs," September 15, 2014, www.dol.gov/ newsroom/releases/eta/eta20141708

13. Ton, Zeynep, "Why 'Good Jobs' Are Good for Retailers," *Harvard Business Review*, January–February 2012. hbr .org/2012/01/why-good-jobs-are-good-for-retailers

14. Department of Labor, "Contingent Workers," 1995 www.dol. gov/dol/aboutdol/history/reich/reports/dunlop/section5.htm

15. Bureau of Labor Statistics, "Contingent and Alternative Employment Arrangements," February 2005 www.bls.gov/news.release/ conemp.toc.htm

16. Katz, Lawrence, F., and Alan B. Krueger, "The Rise and Nature of Alternative Work Arrangements in the United States, 1995-2015," March 29, 2016. krueger.princeton.edu/sites/default/files/ akrueger/files/katz_krueger_cws_-_march_29_20165.pd

17. King, Steve, and Gene Zaino, "Your Company Needs Independent Workers," Harvard Business Review, November 23, 2015. hbr.org/2015/11/your-company-needs-independent-workers, and

Taylor, Timothy, "How Many in the Gig Economy?," Seeking Alpha, February 17, 2016, seekingalpha.com/article/ 3901316-many-gig-economy, and Worstall, Tim, "Contractors and Temps were 100% of Job Growth in the US: And That's a Good Thing, Forbes, March 31, 2016, www.forbes.com/sites/ timworstall/2016/03/31/contractors-and-temps-were-100-of-job-growth-in-us-and-thats-a-good-thing/#4f7610ac1b24, and Sussman, Anna Louise, and Josh Zumbrun, "Contract Workforce Outpaces Growth in Silicon-Valley Style 'Gig' Jobs, WSJ, March 25, 2016, www.wsj.com/articles/contract-workforce-outpaces-growth-in-silicon-valley-style-gig-jobs-1458948608

CHAPTER 1

1. Fox, Jessica, *Three Things You Need to Know About Rockets: A Real-Life Scottish Fairy Tail* (New York: Marble Arch Press, 2013).
2. Campbell, Joseph, The Power of Myth, Anchor Doubleday, 1988.
3. MetLife, "The Do-It-Yourself Dream," 2011 MetLife Study of the American Dream, 2011. www.metlife.com/assets/cao/gbms/ studies/metlife-2011-american-dream-report.pdf
4. The Center for a New American Dream, "New American Dream Survey—A Public Opinion Poll," *The Center for a New American Dream*, 2014. www.newdream.org/resources/poll-2014
5. Kasser, Tim, *The High Price of Materialism* (Cambridge, MA: MIT, 2002).
6. Waldinger, Robert, "What Makes a Good Life? Lessons From the Longest Study on Happiness," *TED.com.* www.ted.com/ talks/robert_waldinger_what_makes_a_good_life_lessons_ from_the_longest_study_on_happiness/transcript?language=en
7. Ware, Bronnie, "Regrets of the Dying," *Bronnie Ware*, November 19, 2009. www.mindful.org/no-regrets/
8. Savage, Roz, *Rowing the Atlantic: Lessons Learned on the Open Ocean* (New York: Simon & Schuster Paperbacks, 2010).
9. Ellis, Linda, "The Dash," *Linda Ellis*, 1996. www.linda-ellis.com/the-dash-the-dash-poem-by-linda-ellis-.html
10. Brooks, David, "The Moral Bucket List," *The New York Times*, April 11, 2015. www.nytimes.com/2015/04/12/opinion/sunday/ david-brooks-the-moral-bucket-list.html
11. Shell, Richard, G., Springboard: Launching Your Personal Search for Success, Penguin Group, August 15, 2013.
12. Gilbert, Daniel Todd, *Stumbling on Happiness* (New York: A.A. Knopf, 2006).

13. Christakis, Nicholas A., and James H. Fowler, *Connected: The Surprising Power of Our Social Networks and How They Shape Our Lives* (New York: Little, Brown, 2011).

14. Groth, Aimee, "You're the Average of the Five People You Spend the Most Time With," Business Insider, July 24, 2012. www.businessinsider.com/jim-rohn-youre-the-average-of-the-five-people-you-spend-the-most-time-with-2012-7

15. Marsh, Nigel, "How to Make Work-Life Balance Work," *TED .com*, May 2010. www.ted.com/talks/nigel_marsh_how_to_make_work_life_balance_work?language=en

16. Christensen, Clayton, "How Will You Measure Your Life?" *Harvard Business Review*, July–August 2012. hbr.org/ 2010/07/how-will-you-measure-your-life

CHAPTER 2

1. Handy, Charles, *The Age of Unreason* (Boston, MA: Harvard Business Review, 1999).

2. Komisar, Randy, and Kent Lineback, *The Monk and the Riddle: The Art of Creating a Life While Making a Living* (Boston, MA: Harvard Business School, 2001).

3. Gladwell, Malcolm, *Outliers: The Story of Success* (New York: Back Bay Books, 2011).

CHAPTER 3

1. Foster, Richard, "Creative Destruction Whips Through Corporate America," *Innosight*, Winter 2012. www.innosight.com/innovation-resources/strategy-innovation/upload/creative-destruction-whips-through-corporate-america_final2015.pdf

2. Daepp, Madeleine I. G., Marcus J. Hamilton, Geoffrey B. West, and Luis M. A. Bettencourt, "The Mortality of Companies," *The Royal Society Publishing*. Santa Fe Institute, April 1, 2015. rsif.royalsocietypublishing.org/content/12/106/20150120

3. Darrow, Barb, "Microsoft Cuts Another 7,800 Jobs, Takes $7.6 Billion 'Impairment Charge,'" *Fortune*, July 8, 2015. fortune.com/2015/07/08/microsoft-layoffs/

4. Brunsman, Barrett, J., "P&G to Eliminate up to 6,000 More Office Jobs," *Cincinnati Business Courier*, April 24, 2015. www.bizjournals.com/cincinnati/news/2015/04/24/p-g-to-eliminate-up-to-6-000-more-office-jobs.html

5. Pramuk, Jacob, "JP Morgan Expected to Cut More Than 5,000 Jobs by Next Year," *CNBC*, May 28, 2015. www.cnbc.com/2015/

05/28/jpmorgan-expected-to-cut-more-than-5000-jobs-by-next-year-dj-citing-sources.html

6. Snyder, Benjamin, "American Express to Cut 4,000 Jobs," *Fortune*, January 21, 2015. fortune.com/2015/01/21/american-express-job-cuts/

7. Moylan, Martin, "For Target, 2015 Brought Layoffs, Empty Shelves and Hope," Minneapolis Public Radio News, December 29, 2015. www.mprnews.org/story/2015/12/29/target-2015-review

8. Wahba, Phil, Walmart CEO tells staff 450 jobs cuts aim to make are to become more 'nimble' retailer, Fortune, October 2, 2015 fortune.com/2015/10/02/walmart-ceo-layoffs/. See also Frost, Peter, "McDonald's lays of 225 as part of cost-cutting," Crain's Chicago Business, August 6, 2015. www.chicagobusiness.com/article/20150806/NEWS07/150809909/mcdonalds-lays-off-225-as-part-of-cost-cutting

9. Oreskovic, Alexei, "Warning Sign: Tech Companies of All Sizes and Ages Are Starting to Have Layoffs," *Business Insider*, October 18, 2015. www.businessinsider.com/tech-company-layoffs-are-increasing-2015-10
See also, Kosoff, Maya, "Groupon Is Laying off 1,100 Employees and Shutting Down its Operations in 7 Countries," *Business Insider*, September 22, 2015. www.businessinsider.com/groupon-laying-off-1100-employees-and-shutting-down-operations-in-7-countries-2015-9

10. Eichler, Alexander, "Government Accounted for Nearly a Third of All Layoffs in 2011: Report," *Huffington Post*, January 5, 2012. www.huffingtonpost.com/2012/01/05/government-finance-layoffs_n_1185938.html

11. University of Pennsylvania, Knowledge@Wharton, "Underfunded Pensions: Tackling an 'Invisible' Crisis," January 26, 2015. knowledge.wharton.upenn.edu/article/underfunded-pensions-tackling-an-invisible-crisis/

12. Glassdoor, Q3 2015 US Employment Confidence Survey. press-content.glassdoor.com/app/uploads/sites/2/2015/10/ECS-Q32015-Supplement.pdf

13. "Employee Job Satisfaction and Engagement," *SHRM*, Society for Human Resource Management, 2015. www.shrm.org/Research/SurveyFindings/Documents/14-0028%20JobSat Engage_Report_FULL_FNL.pdf

14. www.coursera.org, www.edcast.com, www.edx.com, www.novoed.com, www.udemy.com

15. Clark, Dorie, "Reinventing You: Define Your Brand, Imagine

Your Future," Harvard Business Review Press, Boston, April 9, 2013.

16. Topel, Robert H., and Michael P. Ward, "Job Mobility and the Careers of Young Men," *NBER*, The National Bureau for Economic Research, July 1988. www.nber.org/papers/w2649 See also, Keng, Cameron, "Employees Who Stay in Companies Longer than Two Years Get Paid 50% Less," Forbes, June 22, 2014. www.forbes.com/sites/cameronkeng/2014/06/22/employees-that-stay-in-companies-longer-than-2-years-get-paid-50-less/#-3726c14a210e

17. Schoemaker, Paul J. H., and Robert E. Gunther, *Profiting from Uncertainty: Strategies for Succeeding No Matter What the Future Brings* (New York: Atria Press, 2002).

CHAPTER 4

1. Granovetter, Mark S, "The Strength of Weak Ties," *American Journal of Sociology* 78, no. 6. (1973). sociology.stanford.edu/sites/default/files/publications/the_strength_of_weak_ties_and_exch_w-gans.pdf

2. Halligan, Brian, Dharmesh Shah, Inbound Marketing: Get Found Using Google, Social Media and Blogs, Wiley, October 9, 2009.

3. CB Insights, *The Periodic Table of Venture Capital Blogs*, February 10, 2015. www.cbinsights.com/blog/venture-capital-blogs-periodic-table/

4. Cain, Susan, "An Introvert Steps Out," *The New York Times* Sunday Book Review, April 27, 2012. www.nytimes.com/2012/04/29/books/review/how-the-author-of-quiet-delivered-a-rousing-speech.html See also, Cain, Susan, "The Power of Introverts," *TED.com*, www.ted.com/talks/susan_cain_the_power_of_introverts/transcript?language=en

5. Gaignard, Jayson, "Mastermind Dinners: Build Lifelong Relationships by Connecting Experts, Influencers, and Linchpins," Amazon Digital Services *MastermindTalks.com*. December 22, 2104, Web

6. Clark, Dorie, *Stand Out: How to Find Your Breakthrough Idea and Build a Following Around It* (Portfolio, April 21, 2015).

CHAPTER 5

1. Rae, Amber. "Why You Should Scrap that Ladder-Climbing Plan and Go Backpacking Around the World, Instead," *Fast Company*, May 13, 2013. www.fastcompany.com/3009589/why-you-should-scrap-that-ladder-climbing-plan-and-go-backpacking-around-the-world-instead
2. Centers for Disease Control and Prevention, "Injury Prevention and Control: Motor Vehicle Safety - Teen Drivers," October 14, 2015. www.cdc.gov/motorvehiclesafety/teen_drivers/
3. MacMillan, Amanda, "Why Your Commute is Bad For You," CNN, April 6, 2015. www.cnn.com/2015/04/06/health/commute-bad-for-you/
4. Krueger, Norris, Jr., and Peter R. Dickson, "How Believing in Ourselves Increases Risk-Taking: Perceived Self-Efficacy and Opportunity Recognition," *Decision Sciences* 25, no. 3 (1994): 385–400. onlinelibrary.wiley.com/doi/10.1111/j.1540-5915.1994.tb00810.x/abstract
5. Sokol-Hessner, Peter, et al., "Thinking Like a Trader Selectively Reduces Individuals' Loss Aversion," *Proceedings of the National Academy of Sciences* 106, no. 13 (2009). www.pnas.org/content/106/13/5035.full

CHAPTER 6

1. www.habitat.org/getinv/volunteer, ramusa.org/volunteer/, www.appalachiantrail.org/home/volunteer, www.wwoof.net.
2. Kondo, Marie, *The Life-Changing Magic of Tidying Up: The Japanese Art of Decluttering and Organizing* (Berkeley, CA: Ten Speed Press, 2014).
3. Sagmeister, Stefan, "The Power of Time Off," *TED.com*, July 2009. www.ted.com/talks/stefan_sagmeister_the_power_of_time_off/transcript?language=en
4. Slaughter, Anne-Marie, "Why Women Still Can't Have It All," *The Atlantic*, July–August 2012. www.theatlantic.com/magazine/archive/2012/07/why-women-still-cant-have-it-all/309020/
5. Bryson, Bill, *A Walk in the Woods: Rediscovering America on the Appalachian Trail* (New York: Anchor Books).
See also, Strayed, Cheryl, *Wild: From Lost to Found on the Pacific Crest Trail* (New York: Vintage Books, 2013).
6. Kane, Colleen, "These 21 Companies Will Pay You to Take Time Off," *Fortune*, March 16, 2015. fortune.com/2015/03/16/paid-sabbaticals/

7. Tugend, Alina, "Take a Vacation, for Your Health's Sake," *The New York Times*, June 8, 2008. www.nytimes.com/2008/06/08/business/worldbusiness/08iht-07shortcuts.13547623.html?pagewanted=all&_r=1

8. Pinsker, Joe, "41 Percent of American Workers Let Paid Vacation Days Go to Waste," *The Atlantic*, August 22, 2014. www.theatlantic.com/business/archive/2014/08/41-percent-of-american-workers-let-their-paid-vacation-go-to-waste/378950/

9. U.S. Travel Association, "Overwhelmed America: Why Don't We Use Our Earned Leave?" July 2014. www.projecttimeoff.com/sites/default/files/PTO_OverwhelmedAmerica_Report.pdf

10. Nielsen, "The Total Audience Report, Q4 2015," www.nielsen.com/content/dam/corporate/us/en/reports-downloads/2016-reports/q4-2015-total-audience-report.pdf

11. Robinson, Joe, "The Secret to Increased Productivity: Taking Time Off," *Entrepreneur*, September 24, 2014. www.entrepreneur.com/article/237446

12. Sahadi, Jeanne, "These People Took Months Off . . . And it Paid Off Big Time," *CNN Money*, September 12, 2014. money.cnn.com/2014/09/12/pf/time-off-sabbaticals/

13. Chen, Winston, "Leave Work for a Year to Go Live on a Remote Island? How a TED Talk Inspired Me to Take a Mid-Career Sabbatical," *TED Blog*, July 8, 2014. blog.ted.com/how-a-ted-talk-inspired-me-to-take-a-mid-career-sabbatical/

14. Merchant, Nilofer, "In Between Space," July 24, 2014. nilofermerchant.com/2014/07/24/in-between-space/

CHAPTER 7

1. Society for Human Resource Management, "SHRM Survey Findings 2014: Workplace Flexibility: Overview of Flexible Work Arrangements," October 15, 2014. www.shrm.org/research/surveyfindings/articles/pages/2014-workplace-flexibility-survey.aspx

2. Twaronite, Karyn, "Global Generations: A Global Study on Work-Life Challenges Across Generations," *Ernst & Young*. www.ey.com/Publication/vwLUAssets/EY-global-generations/$FILE/EY-global-generations-a-global-study-on-work-life-challenges-across-generations.pdf

3. Vanderkam, Laura, *168 Hours: You Have More Time Than You Think* (London: Penguin, 2011).

4. Bureau of Labor Statistics, American Time Use Survey, 2014. www.bls.gov/tus/charts/leisure.htm

5. Kreider, Tim, "The 'Busy' Trap," *The New York Times*, June 30

2012. opinionator.blogs.nytimes.com/2012/06/30/the-busy-trap/?_r=0

6. Sibonney, Clair, "Arianna Huffington on the Third Metric: You Can Complete a Project by Dropping It," *The Huffington Post*, September 11, 2013. www.huffingtonpost.ca/2013/09/11/arianna-huffington-third-metric_n_3901302.html

7. Graham, Paul, "Maker's Schedule, Manager's Schedule," *Paul Graham*, July 2009. www.paulgraham.com/makersschedule.html

8. Morill, Danielle, "Warming Up to the Manager's Schedule," March 23, 2015. medium.com/@DanielleMorrill/warming-up-to-the-manager-s-schedule-e3ec18c7408e#.gxwnuexbp. Danielle's calendar is reproduced here with permission

9. Seligman, Martin E.P., "Building Resilience," *Harvard Business Review*, April 2011. hbr.org/2011/04/building-resilience

10. Bilger, Burkhard, "The Possibilian," *The New Yorker*, April 25, 2011. www.newyorker.com/magazine/2011/04/25/the-possibilian

11. Chen, Serena and Alice Moon, "The Power to Control Time: Power Influences How Much Time (You Think) You Have," *Journal of Experimental Social Psychology*, April 29, 2014. www.psychologicalscience.org/index.php/news/minds-business/powerful-people-think-they-can-control-time.html

12. Mogilner, Cassie, "You'll Feel Less Rushed if You Give Time Away," *Harvard Business Review*, September 2012. hbr.org/2012/09/youll-feel-less-rushed-if-you-give-time-away

CHAPTER 8

1. U.S. Department of Labor, Bureau of Labor Statistics, Consumer Expenditures—2014, September 3, 2015. www.bls.gov/news.release/pdf/cesan.pdf

2. Rosenberg, Joseph, "Measuring Income for Distributional Analysis," Tax Policy Center, Urban Institute &Brookings Institution, July 25, 2013. www.taxpolicycenter.org/publications/measuring-income-distributional-analysis/full

3. Princeton Survey Research Associates International, "Financial Planning Profiles of American Households: The 2013 Household Financial Planning Survey and Index," *CFP Board of Standards, Inc.*, September 18, 2013. www.cfp.net/docs/public-policy2013-fin-planning-profiles-of-amer-households.pdf

4. CFP Board, "New Research Shows Most American Households Do Financial Planning, but the Extent of this Planning Varies Greatly," September 18, 2013. www.cfp.net/news-events/latest- news/2013/09/18/new-research-shows-most-american-

households-do-financial-planning-but-the-extent-of-this-planning-varies-greatly

CHAPTER 9

1. Gupta, Prerna, "Airbnb Lifestyle: The Rise of the Hipster Nomad," *Tech Crunch*, October 3, 2104. techcrunch.com/2014/10/03/airbnb-lifestyle-the-rise-of-the-hipster-nomad/
2. Federal Reserve Bank of New York, "Quarterly Report on Household Debt and Credit," February 2016. www.newyorkfed.org/medialibrary/interactives/householdcredit/data/pdf/HHDC_2015Q4.pdf
3. Wolff, Edward N., "Household Wealth Trends in the United States, 1962–2013: What Happened over the Great Recession?" *NBER*, The National Bureau of Economic Research, December 2014. www.nber.org/papers/w20733
4. Pew Research Center, "The American Middle Class Is Losing Ground: No Longer the Majority and Falling Behind Financially," Washington, D.C., December 2015. www.pewsocialtrends.org/files/2015/12/2015-12-09_middle-class_FINAL-report.pdf
5. Yale economist Robert Shiller analyzed home prices and concluded that "From 1890 to 1990, real inflation-corrected home prices were virtually unchanged." www.cnbc.com/2014/12/08/where-to-put-your-cash-a-house-or-a-stock.html and www.usatoday.com/story/money/personalfinance/2014/05/10/why-your-home-is-not-a-good-investment/8900911/. Shiller's housing market data is found at www.econ.yale.edu/~shiller/data.htm
   See also, Robert Shiller, "Buying a House is a 'Consumption Choice,' Not an Investment," theweek.com/speedreads/563510/economist-robert-shiller-buying-house-consumption-choice-not-investment
6. Wolff, Edward N., "Household Wealth Trends in the United States, 1962–2013: What Happened over the Great Recession?" *NBER*, The National Bureau of Economic Research, December 2014. www.nber.org/papers/w20733
7. Urban-Brookings Tax Policy Center, "Statistics: Type of Deduction 1999–2013," December 15, 2015. www.taxpolicycenter.org/statistics/type-deduction
8. Toder, Eric J., "Options to Reform the Home Mortgage Interest Deduction," *Tax Policy Center*, Urban-Brookings Tax Policy Center, April 25, 2013. www.taxpolicycenter.org/

publications/options-reform-deduction-home-mortgage-interest-0/full

See also, Testimony Before the Committee on Ways and Means, United States House of Representatives, Hearing on Tax Reform and Real Estate, April 25, 2013. waysandmeans.house.gov/UploadedFiles/Toder_Testimony_42513_fc.pdf

9. Federal Reserve Bank of St. Louis, Economic Research, December 2015. research.stlouisfed.org/fred2/series/MSPNHSUS

10. The Joint Center for Housing Studies, "America's Rental Housing: Expanding Options for Diverse and Growing Demand," December 9, 2015. jchs.harvard.edu/americas-rental-housing

11. Rent vs. buy a home: www.nytimes.com/interactive/2014/upshot/buy-rent-calculator.html, www.zillow.com/rent-vs-buy-calculator/
See also, Rent vs. buy a car: www.zipcar.com/is-it#savingsversusownership.

12. Roberts, David, "Our Year of Living Airbnb," *The New York Times*, November 25, 2015. www.nytimes.com/2015/11/29/realestate/our-year-of-living-airbnb.html

13. Pew Research Center, February 2014, "The Rising Cost of Not Going to College," www.pewsocialtrends.org/files/2014/02/SDT-higher-ed-FINAL-02-11-2014.pdf
See also, Hershbein, Brad, and Melissa Kearney, "Major Decisions: What Graduates Earn over Their Lifetimes," *The Hamilton Project*, September 29, 2104. www.hamiltonproject.org/assets/legacy/files/downloads_and_links/Major_Decisions_Lifetime_Earnings_by_Major.pdf
See also, U.S. Department of Education, Institute of Education Sciences, National Center for Education Statistics, "Annual Earnings of Young Adults," 2015. nces.ed.gov/fastfacts/display.asp?id=77

14. Davis, Alyssa, Will Kimball, Elise Gould, "The Class of 2015: Despite an Improving Economy, Young Grads Still Face an Uphill Climb," Economic Policy Institute, briefing paper #401, May 27, 2015. www.epi.org/files/2015/the-class-of-2015-revised.pdf

15. Federal Register, February 19, 2003, Vol. 68, No. 33, 8141–8152, www2.ed.gov/legislation/FedRegister/finrule/2003-1/021903a.html

16. Iuliano, Jason, "An Empirical Assessment of Student Loan Discharges and the Undue Hardship Standard," *American Bankruptcy Law Journal* 86 (September 25, 2012): 495–526. papers.ssrn.com/sol3/papers.cfm?abstract_id=189444517

17. nomoreharvarddebt.com

18. Bernard, Tara Siegel, "Medical, Dental, 401(k)? Now Add School Loan Aid to Job Benefits," *New York Times*, March 25 2016. www.nytimes.com/2016/03/26/your-money/medical-dental-401-k-now-add-school-loan-aid-to-job-benefits.tml?_r=1

19. Ernst & Young, "EY Transforms Its Recruitment Selection Process for Graduates, Undergraduates and School Leavers," August 3, 2015. www.ey.com/UK/en/Newsroom/News-releases/ 15-08-03—EY-transforms-its-recruitment-selection-process-for-graduates-undergraduates-and-school-leavers

CHAPTER 10

1. The Pew Charitable Trusts, "The State Pensions Funding Gap: Challenges Persist," July 14, 2015. www.pewtrusts.org/en/research-and-analysis/issue-briefs/2015/07/the-state-pensions-funding-gap-challenges-persist

2. Internal Revenue Service, "Retirement Plans for Self-Employed People," December 17, 2015. www.irs.gov/retirement-plans/retirement-plans-for-self-employed-people

3. I used both Vanguard and Fidelity online calculators to estimate the contribution amounts for a simple example. Exact amounts would depend on specific factors, so to estimate your own contribution amounts, talk to an accountant or financial planner. personal.vanguard.com/us/SbsCalculatorController?FW_Event=chgBusType&NavStep=1scs.fidelity.com/products/mobile/sepMobile.shtm

4. Plan Sponsor Council of America, "PSCA's 57th Annual Survey Validates the Success of the Defined Contribution System," December3,2014.www.psca.org/psca-s-57th-annual-survey-validates-the-success-of-the-defined-contribution-system

5. Internal Revenue Service, "Retirement Topics—IRA Contribution Limits," www.irs.gov/Retirement-Plans/Plan-Participant,-Employee/Retirement-Topics-IRA-Contribution-Limits

6. Garon, Sheldon, *Beyond Our Means: Why America Spends While the World Saves*: (Princeton, NJ: Princeton University Press, 2013).

7. Schrager, Allison, "American Is Full of High-Earning Poor People." *Quartz*, November 3, 2015. qz.com/520414/the-high-earning-poor/

8. Employee Benefit Research Institute and Greenwald & Associates, Retirement Confidence Survey, "2016 RCS Fact Sheet #3: Preparing for Retirement in America," www.ebri.org/files/RCS15.FS-3.Preps2.pdf

9. "Wells Fargo Retirement Study: A Few Years Makes a Big

Difference," October 22, 2105. www.wellsfargo.com/about/
press/2015/few-years-difference_1022/

10. Health View Insights, "Health View Services: 2015 Retirement
Health Care Costs Data Report," 2015. www.hvsfinancial.com/
PublicFiles/Data_Release.pdf

11. Rhee, Nari, and Ilana Boivie, "The Continuing Retirement
Savings Crisis," National Institute on Retirement Security,
March 2015, laborcenter.berkeley.edu/pdf/2015/Retirement
SavingsCrisis.pdf
See also, Harrison, David, "The Biggest Reason Workers Don't
Save for Retirement," *Wall Street Journal*, September 29, 2015,
blogs.wsj.com/economics/2015/09/29/the-biggest-reason-workers-
dont-save-for-retirement/

12. American Benefits Institute and WorldatWork, "Trends in 401(k)
Plans and Retirement Rewards," March 2013. www.american-
benefitscouncil.org/pub/e613e2a9-cb3b-b159-6cff-6931bd1953a6
See also, Butrica, Barbara, and Nadia Karamcheva, "Automatic
Enrollment, Employer Match Rates, and Employee Compensation in 401(k) Plans," *Monthly Labor Review*, May 2015.
www.bls.gov/opub/mlr/2015/article/automatic-enrollment-employer-
match-rates-and-employee-compensation-in-401k-plans.htm

13. Vanguard, "How America Saves 2014: A Report on Vanguard
2013 Defined Contribution Plan Results," June 2014. pressroom
.vanguard.com/content/nonindexed/How_America_Saves_2014
.pdf

14. Munnell, Alice, Annika Sunden, and Catherine Taylor, "What
Determines 401(k) Participation and Contributions?" Social
Security Office of Policy, *Social Security Bulletin* 64, no. 3
(2001/2002). www.ssa.gov/policy/docs/ssb/v64n3/v64n3p64
.html

15. Goda, Gopi Shah, et al., "The Role of Time Preferences and
Exponential-Growth Bias in Retirement Savings," 17th Annual
Joint Meeting of the Retirement Research Consortium, Washington, D.C., August 6–7, 2015. www.nber.org/programs/ag/rrc/
rrc2015/papers/7.1%20-%20Goda,%20Levy,%20Manchester,
%20Sojourner,%20Tasoff.pdf

16. Certified Financial Planner Board of Standards and the Consumer Federation of America, "Financial Planning Profiles of
American Households: The 2013 Household Financial Planning
Survey and Index," September 18, 2013. www.cfp.net/docs/public-
policy/2013-fin-planning-profiles-of-amer-households.pdf

17. Pew Research Center, "The American Middle Class Is Losing
Ground," December 9, 2015. www.pewsocialtrends.org/
files/2015/12/2015-12-09_middle-class_FINAL-report.pdf

18. Accenture, "The 'Greater' Wealth Transfer: Capitalizing on the Intergenerational Shift in Wealth," 2015. www.accenture.com/us-en/~/media/Accenture/Conversion-Assets/DotCom/Documents/Global/PDF/Industries_5/Accenture-CM-AWAMS-Wealth-Transfer-Final-June2012-Web-Version.pdf
19. Ibid. "The 'Greater' Wealth Transfer," *Accenture*, 2015. www.accenture.com/us-en/~/media/Accenture/Conversion-Assets/Dot Com/Documents/Global/PDF/Industries_5/Accenture-CM-AWAMS-Wealth-Transfer-Final-June2012-Web-Version.pdf
20. Helman, Ruth, Craig Copeland, and Jack VanDerhei, "The 2016 Retirement Confidence Survey: Worker Confidence Stable, Retiree Confidence Continues to Increase," Employee Benefit Research Institute, April 2016. www.ebri.org/files/RCS_16 .FS-2_Expects1.pdf
21. Wells Fargo, "Wells Fargo Retirement Study: A Few Years Makes a Big Difference," October 22, 2015. www08 .wellsfargomedia.com/assets/pdf/commercial/retirement-employee-benefits/perspectives/2015-retirement-study.pdf
22. Employee Benefit Research Institute and Greenwald & Associates, Retirement Confidence Survey, "2016 RCS Fact Sheet #2: Expectations about Retirement in America," www.ebri.org/files/RCS_16.FS-2_Expects1.pdf
23. Wells Fargo, "Wells Fargo Retirement Study: A Few Years Makes a Big Difference," October 22, 2015. www08.wellsfargomedia .com/assets/pdf/commercial/retirement-employee-benefits/perspectives/2015-retirement-study.pdf
24. The Henry J. Kaiser Family Foundation, "2015 Employer Health Benefits Survey," September 22, 2015. kff.org/report-section/ehbs-2015-section-eleven-retiree-health-benefits/
25. Author Tim Ferriss is credited with introducing the term "mini-retirement" in his book *The 4-Hour Workweek*.

THE FUTURE GIG ECONOMY

1. U.S. Senate Committee on Health, Education, Labor, and Pensions, U.S. Department of Labor, "Statement of Seth D. Harris Deputy Secretary U.S. Department of Labor Before the Committee on Health, Education, Labor, and Pensions," June 17, 2010. www.dol.gov/_sec/media/congress/20100617_Harris.htm
2. Carre, Francoise, "(In)dependent Contractor Misclassification," Economic Policy Institute, June 8, 2015. www.epi.org/publication/independent-contractor-misclassification/

3. IRS, "Independent Contractor (Self-Employed) or Employee?" www.irs.gov/Businesses/Small-Businesses-&-Self-Employed/ Independent-Contractor-Self-Employed-or-Employee

4. U.S. Department of Labor, "Administrator's Interpretation No. 2015-1," July 15, 2015. www.dol.gov/whd/workers/ misclassification/AI-2015_1.htm

5. www.employmentlawspotlight.com/2014/10/nlrb-adopts-new-test-for-independent-contractor-misclassification-applies-it-to-find-fedex-drivers-are-employees-who-can-unionize/

6. Christian, Blake E., "IRS Compliance and Enforcement Trends," *Journal of Accountancy*, September 2012. www.journalofaccountancy.com/issues/2012/sep/20125947 .html

7. Center on Budget and Policy Priorities, "Policy Basics: Where do Federal Tax Revenues Come From?," March 4, 2016. www.cbpp.org/research/policy-basics-where-do-federal-tax-revenues-come-from

8. Hanauer, Nick, and David Rolf, "Shared Security, Shared Growth," *Democracy Journal,* no. 27, Summer 2015. democracy-journal.org/magazine/37/shared-security-shared-growth/

9. Ip, Greg, "As the Gig Economy Changes, So Should the Rules," WSJ, December 9, 2015. www.wsj.com/articles/as-the-gig-economy-changes-work-so-should-rules- 1449683384
See also, Weber, Lauren, "What if There Were a New Type of Worker? Dependent Contractor," WSJ, January 28, 2015. www.wsj.com/articles/what-if-there-were-a-new-type-of-worker-dependent-contractor-1422405831
See also, Haigu, Andrei, and Rob Biederman, "The Dawning of the Age of Flex Labor," *Harvard Business Review*, September 4, 2015. hbr.org/2015/09/the-age-of-flex-labor-is-here
See also, Cruz, Roberto, "A Class of Their Own? Independent Contractors Causing a Conundrum," Workforce, September 1, 2015 www.workforce.com/articles/21560-a-class-of-their-own-independent-contractors-causing-conundrum

10. Kitces, Michael, "Why Employee Benefits Will Become Irrelevant," *The Wall Street Journal*, April 28, 2015. blogs.wsj.com/ experts/2015/04/28/why-employee-benefits-will-become-irrelevant/

11. Hanauer, Nick, and David Rolf, "Shared Security, Shared Growth," *Democracy Journal,* no. 27, Summer 2015. democracy-journal.org/magazine/37/shared-security-shared-growth/

12. Hill, Steven, "The Future of Work in the Uber Economy," *Boston Review*, July 22, 2015. bostonreview.net/us/steven-hill-uber-economy-individual-security-accounts

13. Reich, Robert, "The Upsurge in Uncertain Work," *Robert Reich,* August 23, 2015. robertreich.org/post/127426324745

14. Reich, Robert, "Inequality for All Q&A" (video). www.dailykos .com/story/2014/3/26/1287365/-Robert-Reich-Universal-Basic-Income-In-The-US-Almost-Inevitable

15. Harford, Tim, "An Economist's Dreams of a Fairer Gig Economy," *Tim Harfor,* December 29, 2015. next.ft.com/ content/1280a92e-a405-11e5-873f-68411a84f346Web

16. Beekman, Daniel, "The Seattle City Council Voted 8-0 Monday Afternoon to Enact Councilmember Mike O'Brien's Ordinance, Giving Taxi, For-Hire and Uber Drivers the Ability to Unionize," December 16, 2015. www.seattletimes.com/seattle-news/ politics/unions-for-taxi-uber-drivers-seattle-council-votes-today/

17. Somerville, Heather, and Dan Levine, "US Chamber of Commerce Sues Seattle over Uber, Lyft Ordinance," Reuters, March 3, 2016. www.reuters.com/article/us-uber-tech-seattle-chamberofcommerce-idUSKCN0W52SD

18. Gallup, "What Everyone in the World Wants: A Good Job," June 9, 2015 www.gallup.com/businessjournal/183527/everyone-world-wants-good-job.aspx

19. Ton, Zeynep, "Why 'Good Jobs' are Good for Retailers," *Harvard Business Review,* January-February 2012. issue. hbr.org/2012/01/why-good-jobs-are-good-for-retailers

20. Hill, Steven, *How the "Uber Economy" and Runaway Capitalism are Screwing American Workers* (New York: St. Martin's Press, 2015).

21. Csikszentmihalyi, Mihaly, *Flow: The Psychology of Optimal Experience* (New York: Harper Perennial, 2008).

INDEX

ABOUT THE AUTHOR

Diane created and teaches The Gig Economy, which was named by *Forbes* as one of the Top 10 Most Innovative Business School Classes in the country. She is an Adjunct Lecturer in the MBA program at Babson College and a Senior Fellow at the Ewing Marion Kauffman Foundation.

Diane is an active and enthusiastic participant in The Gig Economy. In between full-time jobs and consulting gigs, Diane has been a Visiting Fellow at Trinity College in Dublin, an Executive-in-Residence at Babson College, and an Eisenhower Fellow. She has written and published two books and a widely read report on the venture capital. Her work has been featured in The Economist, Forbes, Fortune, Harvard Business Review, The New Yorker, The Wall Street Journal, as well as numerous industry publications. Diane has freelanced several articles and commentary pieces, taken two different years off to travel around the world, and lived in five different cities.

When not working, she loves reading (mostly nonfiction), writing (only nonfiction), food (eating and cooking), wine, yoga, and running. Diane holds undergraduate and graduate degrees from Harvard University, and is a dual U.S. and Irish citizen.

Visit her at
www.dianemulcahy.com
and follow her on
Twitter @dianemulcahy